Cooking

with

BONNIE STERN

Random House of Canada

Canadian Cataloguing in Publication Data

Stern, Bonnie
   Cooking with Bonnie Stern

Rev. ed.
Previously published under title: The Bonnie Stern cookbook
ISBN: 0-679-30813-X

1. Cookery. I. Title. II. Title: Bonnie Stern Cookbook

TX715.S772 1996   641.5   C96-930773-X

Editor: Shelley Tanaka
Cover design: Andrew Smith
Interior design and page composition: Joseph Gisini / Andrew Smith Graphics Inc.
Cover photograph of Bonnie Stern: Lorella Zanetti
Illustrations: Bo-Kim Louie and David Mazierski

Printed and bound in Canada

10 9 8 7 6 5 4 3 2 1

For Mark, Anna and Fara,
and for all the other special children who inspired
this book

CONTENTS

Contents

INTRODUCTION

Ten years ago, I became involved in a wonderful project, *The CKFM Bonnie Stern Cookbook*. It grew out of a weekly radio spot that I did on CKFM's (now called The Mix 99.9) "Hour Toronto Magazine." It was a unique program that combined hard news and public affairs with contributions from some pretty eclectic regulars—Jeremy Brown, Brian Costello, Don Daynard, Norm Forman, Barbara Klich and me—all cheerfully kept in line by our producer Peter Pacini and hosts Dave Agar and Judy Webb. With Judy, I got to talk about my favourite subject—food—and share some of my favourite recipes with listeners.

Talking about food on the radio presented some pretty special challenges for someone who was used to demonstrating recipes in a cooking school classroom or on TV—like the time I tried to describe a particular way to cut asparagus (see page 97), or how to roll out pastry without making it look like a map of Norway with fjords on all sides.

But listeners didn't seem to mind. One woman told us that she had heard the show while stuck in traffic, and she'd ended up copying down the recipe with lipstick on a Kleenex. We didn't want to cause any accidents, so after that we started mailing out copies. But it was still a pretty complicated way to collect recipes.

So, in 1986, to celebrate the show's tenth anniversary, the station asked me to put together a cookbook of the recipes most requested by listeners. All proceeds from the sale of the book were to go to the CKFM Children's Fund in support of the Hospital for Sick Children.

The book really became a labour of love. Astro Dairy Products, the makers of excellent yogurts, cream cheese and sour cream, offered to sponsor the publication of the book. And a wonderful team from CKFM, Somerville House, Random House and my own staff at the cooking school joined together to create a book that many of my students tell me is still one of the most well-used cookbooks in their kitchens.

Last spring I was asked to revise and update that book. I've been happy to see how well my old favourites have stood up—food fashion will never eliminate the need for the greatest rice pudding recipe of all time (see page 168). I've added several new recipes, too—Thai and Southwest dishes, beans and legumes, comforting and economical stews. Also, I've been teaching low-fat classes for decades, and my recent collaboration with the Heart and Stroke Foundation has focussed on the benefits of healthful cooking, so, where I could do so without affecting taste, I've reduced the fat and salt in the original recipes. I've also provided low-fat alternatives where appropriate, but don't forget that many of the recipes are already low in fat. On the other hand, some are very rich and cannot be changed without significantly altering the taste; in those cases I think it's better to eat small portions rather than trying to use substitutions.

I want to thank again the team that worked on the original book, the radio listeners who made it possible, the children who inspired it, and the people who bought the book to raise money for the hospital. Thanks also to the people at Random House of Canada, my faithful cooking students, my hard-working, patient staff, and, as always, my loving and supportive family.

Bonnie Stern
September, 1996

APPETIZERS

OLIVE MUSTARD SPREAD

This is a wonderful spread for French bread or crackers, but it can also be served as a sauce with cold cuts. It can be used directly from the refrigerator, but it is creamier at room temperature.

I like to use The Original Canadian Beer Mustard in this recipe, but any coarse-grained mustard will do. And try to use good-quality European olives, such as Kalamata. They must be pitted (smash the olives with the side of a knife to loosen the pits), but their flavour is far superior to most canned, pitted olives.

MAKES APPROX. 1½ CUPS/375 ML

1½ cups	black olives, pitted	375 mL
2 tbsp	coarse-grained mustard	25 mL
½	small red onion, chopped	½
2 tbsp	chopped fresh basil or parsley	25 mL
½ tsp	freshly ground pepper	2 mL
¼ cup	unsalted butter, at room temperature	50 mL

1. Place the pitted olives in a food processor or blender and process until finely chopped.

2. Add the remaining ingredients and process until smooth. Taste and adjust the seasonings if necessary.

   LOWER-FAT VERSION: *Use low-fat pressed cottage cheese or yogurt cheese (see page 28) instead of the butter.*

SMOKED SALMON CANAPÉS

This is a great way to use up little bits of leftover smoked salmon. Serve the canapés for snacks or as an appetizer, or use the salmon mixture in sandwiches.

MAKES APPROX. 30 CANAPÉS

8 oz	smoked salmon	250 g
¼ cup	unsalted butter, at room temperature	50 mL
½ cup	ricotta cheese, well drained	125 mL
2 tbsp	lemon juice	25 mL
	Pumpernickel	
	Sprigs fresh dill	
1 oz	salmon caviar (optional)	30 g
	Lemon slices	

1. Chop the smoked salmon in a food processor or mince finely with a knife.

2. Combine the salmon and butter until smooth. Blend in the ricotta cheese and lemon juice. (Add pepper if you wish.)

3. Cut the pumpernickel into 1½-inch/4 cm squares or rounds and pipe or spoon the salmon mixture on them.

4. Decorate with a sprig of dill or a few drops of salmon caviar. Place on a serving platter and garnish with lemon slices.

LOWER-FAT VERSION: *Use ¾ cup/175mL light ricotta instead of the butter and the regular ricotta.*

SMOKED SALMON PÂTÉ

When you serve anything made with smoked salmon, guests feel special. Smoked salmon is rich, elegant and luxurious in texture, with a price to match. When you use it in this recipe, however, a small amount of salmon serves a lot of people, and your guests will still feel special.

This recipe will serve 12 to 16 people, but it can also be halved.

MAKES I LOAF

I	envelope unflavoured gelatine	I
¼ cup	cold water	50 mL
I cup	whipping cream	250 mL
12 oz	smoked salmon, diced	375 g
4 oz	cream cheese	125 g
I cup	sour cream	250 mL
2 tbsp	lemon juice	25 mL
	Salt and freshly ground pepper to taste	
10 oz	spinach, cooked and squeezed dry	300 g
	Lemon slices, tomato roses and/or watercress	

1. Sprinkle the gelatine over the cold water in a small saucepan. Allow it to rest for 5 minutes. Heat gently and stir to dissolve the gelatine.

2. Whip the cream lightly until soft peaks form. Reserve.

3. Place the smoked salmon in a food processor fitted with the steel knife (this can also be done in a blender). Chop the smoked salmon coarsely.

4. Add the cream cheese and blend until the cream cheese is smooth. Add the sour cream and blend well. Blend in the lemon juice, salt and pepper (the amount of salt you add will depend on the saltiness of the salmon).

5. Add the gelatine to the mixture in the food processor or blender and combine well.

6. Add all but a few spoonfuls of the mixture to the whipped cream and fold in gently but thoroughly. Taste and adjust the seasonings.

7. Add the spinach to the remaining salmon mixture in the food processor or blender and blend well. Taste and adjust the seasonings.

8. Line an 8- x 4-inch/1.5 L loaf pan with plastic wrap. Add half the salmon mixture and spread out evenly. Spread all of the spinach mixture over that. Top with remaining salmon mixture.

9. Cover with plastic wrap and refrigerate for at least 3 hours. Unmould onto a pretty loaf plate and decorate with lemon slices, tomato roses (see page 21) and/or watercress.

   LOWER-FAT VERSION: *Use light cream cheese and light sour cream. Use yogurt cheese (see page 28) instead of the whipped cream.*

CRÊPES WITH SMOKED SALMON AND CREAM CHEESE

This is a very elegant appetizer. If you have difficulty making crêpes in a traditional omelette or crêpe pan, use a non-stick pan or a specially designed "upside-down" crêpe pan.

SERVES 6 (12 CRÊPES)

CRÊPES

4	eggs	4
I cup	all-purpose flour	250 mL
½ tsp	salt	2 mL
I tbsp	granulated sugar	15 mL
I cup	milk	250 mL
¼ cup	water	50 mL
I tbsp	unsalted butter, melted	15 mL

FILLING

12 oz	cream cheese	375 g
2 tbsp	lemon juice	25 mL
¼ cup	finely chopped fresh dill	50 mL
	Salt and freshly ground pepper to taste	
I lb	smoked salmon, thinly sliced	500 g

1. Prepare the crêpe batter by combining all the crêpe ingredients. Let rest, covered, for 1 hour.

2. Heat an 8-inch/20 cm non-stick crêpe or omelette pan. Brush with 1 tbsp/15 mL additional unsalted butter (unsalted butter burns and sticks less easily than salted butter). Make the crêpes by adding a ladleful of batter. Swirl it in the pan and pour the excess batter back into the batter bowl. Cook the crêpe until brown, then flip. Cook the second side. Repeat with the remaining batter (you should have about 12 crêpes).

3. To make the filling, combine the cheese, lemon juice and dill. Add salt and pepper to taste. Spread filling on each crêpe and arrange two slices of salmon on each. Fold each crêpe in half and then in quarters (see illustration).

4. Serve two crêpes per person as an appetizer, or serve like party sandwiches for hors d'oeuvres.

LOWER-FAT VERSION: *Use low-fat milk in the crêpes. Use light cream cheese or yogurt cheese (see page 28) instead of regular cream cheese.*

Muffuletta Olive Salad

This popular New Orleans olive salad is the base for the city's most famous sandwich. The sandwich is made with a large, flat sesame bun, a variety of sliced meats and cheeses and then topped with this salad.

You can also use this salad as part of an antipasto platter, serve it as a spread with ham or salami sandwiches, or toss it with 1 ½ lb/750 g cooked pasta and serve it hot or cold. Or toss with 2 lb/1 kg cooked red potatoes for a wonderful potato salad.

MAKES APPROX. 3 CUPS/750 ML

2 cups	green olives stuffed with pimentos	500 mL
½ cup	black olives, pitted	125 mL
I	4-oz/125 g jar marinated artichokes	I
2 tbsp	diced pimento	25 mL
I tbsp	finely chopped hot pickled peppers	15 mL
2 tbsp	pickled pepper juice	25 mL
½ tsp	dried oregano	2 mL
½ tsp	freshly ground pepper	2 mL
2	cloves garlic, minced	2
2	anchovy fillets, minced	2
2 tbsp	capers	25 mL
¼ cup	olive oil	50 mL

1. Smash the olives and chop them coarsely. Chop the artichokes and combine with the olives (use the juices of the artichokes as well).

2. Add all the remaining ingredients and combine well. This can be done in a food processor but be careful not to puree completely—pulse ingredients on/off just until the mixture is semi-pureed. Taste and adjust seasonings if necessary.

HUNDRED CORNER SHRIMP BALLS

These little dim sum treats are so delicious and very easy to prepare. They are great hot or at room temperature and can be served with a dipping sauce of hot chili sauce or salt seasoned with a little curry powder, five-spice powder or crushed Szechuan peppercorns. They can be made ahead and reheated in the oven.

Any white-fleshed fish fillets can be used instead of the shrimp. The shrimp paste itself (without the bread cubes) can also be poached in water and served as dumplings in soup, or can be panfried as little shrimp patties.

MAKES APPROX. 3 DOZEN BALLS

12	slices white bread	12
1 lb	raw shrimp, shelled and cleaned	500 g
1	egg white	1
1 tbsp	rice wine	15 mL
1 tsp	salt	5 mL
1 tsp	finely chopped ginger root	5 mL
1 tbsp	finely chopped green onion	15 mL
¼ cup	finely chopped water chestnuts	50 mL
2 tbsp	cornstarch	25 mL
4 cups	peanut oil for deep-frying	1 L

1. Remove the crusts from the bread. Dice the bread into ¼-inch/5 mm cubes. Place on a baking sheet and dry out in a very low oven (200°F/90°C) for about 30 minutes.

2. Pat the shrimp dry and mince in a food processor or blender. Blend in all the remaining ingredients except the oil.

3. With wet hands, shape the shrimp paste into 1-inch/2.5 cm balls and roll in the bread cubes. Press the cubes firmly into the shrimp mixture.

4. Heat the oil in a wok or deep, wide pot to 375°F/190°C. Cook the shrimp balls in batches until nicely browned and cooked through (this should only take 4 to 5 minutes). Drain on paper towels.

LOWER-FAT VERSION: *Omit the bread. Poach the shrimp balls in water for about 5 minutes, or just until cooked. Serve as dumplings in soup or with hot sauce as an appetizer.*

CHÈVRE SPREAD

This flavourful, tangy spread is great served with bread or crackers. It can also be piped into mushroom caps, cherry tomatoes, cucumber slices or Belgian endive leaves. Buy soft, unripened goat cheese for this recipe, preferably without a rind.

MAKES APPROX. 2 CUPS/500 ML

12 oz	chèvre (goat cheese), rind removed	375 g
½ cup	unsalted butter, at room temperature	125 mL
1	small clove garlic, minced	1
½ tsp	Tabasco sauce	2 mL
¼ tsp	dried thyme	1 mL
¼ tsp	dried rosemary	1 mL
¼ tsp	freshly ground pepper	1 mL
2 tbsp	finely chopped black olives	25 mL
2 tbsp	finely chopped sun-dried tomatoes	25 mL

1. Cream the chèvre with the butter until smooth.

2. Blend in the garlic, Tabasco, thyme, rosemary and pepper.

3. Stir in the olives and tomatoes. (Do not blend because you want them to remain as little colourful pieces suspended in the mixture.)

   LOWER-FAT VERSION: *Use yogurt cheese (see page 28) instead of butter and omit olives.*

Cajun Spiced Almonds

These very spicy almonds will wake up your appetite before dinner, and they are delicious as a snack any time. Don't serve too many, though, as it is very hard to stop eating them! The idea to glaze the nuts with corn syrup came from Abby Mandel, who is well known throughout North America for her food-processor recipes. The nuts are not sweet, but glazed beautifully.

These can also be frozen. If they are not crisp enough, rebake for 15 minutes before serving. For a less spicy version use half the cayenne, Tabasco sauce and pepper.

MAKES APPROX. 3 CUPS/750 ML

2 tbsp	unsalted butter	25 mL
¼ cup	corn syrup	50 mL
2 tbsp	water	25 mL
1½ tsp	salt	7 mL
1 tsp	cayenne pepper	5 mL
2 tsp	paprika	10 mL
2 tsp	Tabasco sauce	10 mL
1 tsp	freshly ground pepper	5 mL
1 lb	whole almonds with skins	500 g

1. Preheat the oven to 250°F/120°C. Line a baking sheet with aluminum foil or parchment paper.

2. Place the butter, corn syrup, water, salt, cayenne, paprika, Tabasco and pepper in a heavy saucepan. Bring to a boil.

3. Stir in the almonds and coat them well.

4. Spread the almonds on the baking sheet and bake for 1 hour. Stir every 15 minutes to separate the nuts.

GRILLED CARPACCIO SALAD

Carpaccio is an Italian specialty where the meat is usually served raw. In this version, the meat is coated with a mustard glaze and cooked briefly but served very rare. If you prefer meat more well done, cook it a little longer.

This can be served as an appetizer or for a special lunch. The recipe calls for more filet than you will need for eight servings. However, if you use less, it will be almost impossible to slice it all very thin. Use up any extra in salads or sandwiches.

SERVES 8

2 lb	filet roast, trimmed	1 kg
3 tbsp	Dijon mustard	45 mL
1 tsp	Worcestershire sauce	5 mL
1 tsp	soy sauce	5 mL
8	large leaves ruby lettuce or radicchio	8
4 oz	fresh mushrooms, thinly sliced	125 g
4 oz	Parmigiano Reggiano, thinly sliced	125 g
2 tbsp	lemon juice	25 mL
⅓ cup	olive oil	75 mL
½ tsp	salt	2 mL
¼ tsp	freshly ground pepper	1 mL

1. Preheat the oven to 450°F/225°C. Pat the filet dry.

2. Combine the mustard with the Worcestershire and soy sauce. Spread this mixture over the filet. Place the filet on a roasting rack and roast for 10 minutes. Remove from the oven and cool. (The roast will be very rare.) Freeze for 40 minutes for easier slicing.

3. With a very sharp carving knife, slice the filet very, very thin.

4. On each serving plate arrange a leaf of lettuce. Arrange a few slices of the filet on top. Decorate with the mushrooms and thin slices of cheese, but allow some of the filet to show through.

5. Combine the lemon juice, olive oil, salt and pepper and drizzle over the salad.

OLIVADA AND MASCARPONE TORTA

This layered cheese spread is a spectacular company treat. Serve it with French bread and/or crackers. Any leftovers can easily be made into sandwiches. I have even tossed this mixture with cooked fettuccine and Parmesan cheese for a sensational pasta dish.

Mascarpone is a creamy Italian cheese that is becoming more and more available in North America. If you cannot find mascarpone, use 1 lb/500 g ricotta cheese blended with 1 cup/250 mL unsalted butter as a substitute.

Another great version of this can be made using a half recipe of pesto sauce (see page 85) instead of the olivada.

MAKES APPROX. 3 CUPS/750 ML

1	clove garlic, minced	1
2 tbsp	minced red onion	25 mL
3 tbsp	minced fresh parsley or basil	45 mL
1½ cups	black olives, pitted and coarsely chopped	375 mL
½ tsp	freshly ground pepper	2 mL
½ cup	unsalted butter, at room temperature	125 mL
1½ lb	mascarpone cheese	750 g
	Fresh basil and tomato roses for garnish	

1. To make the olivada, combine the garlic, onion, parsley, olives, pepper and butter in a food processor or blender. Blend until you have a paste-like mixture.

2. Line a 4-cup/1 L soufflé dish or mould with plastic wrap.

3. Beat the cheese until smooth.

4. Spread one-quarter of the mascarpone in the bottom of the mould. Top with one-third of the olivada. Continue layering until the cheese and olive mixtures are used up, ending with a cheese layer.

5. Wrap well in plastic wrap and refrigerate for a few hours or overnight.

6. To serve, unwrap and unmould on a serving plate. Garnish with basil leaves and tomato roses (see illustration).

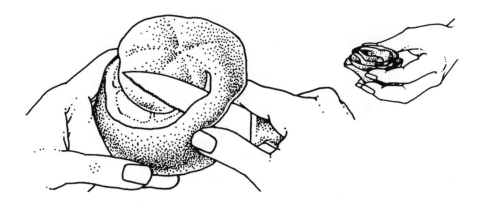

SMOKED TROUT TARTARE

When Jacques Pépin teaches at my school, he always causes a sensation. Not only does he teach delicious recipes and excellent cooking techniques, he is also perfectly charming—students fall in love with him immediately. When he leaves, everyone (even the worn-out staff) rushes home to prepare his recipes.

This recipe is based on one of his dishes. He used fresh raw salmon, but I like to use smoked salmon or smoked trout instead. That way, even fussy eaters will love it.

You can use this as a spread with black bread, crackers or buttered toast, or serve it in Belgian endive leaves or hollowed-out cucumber slices.

MAKES APPROX. 5 DOZEN HORS D'OEUVRES

4	smoked trout (about 8 oz/250 g each)	4
1 tbsp	olive oil	15 mL
¼ cup	lemon juice	50 mL
½ tsp	grated lemon peel	2 mL
¼ cup	chopped fresh chives or green onions	50 mL
¼ cup	chopped fresh parsley	50 mL
¼ cup	chopped fresh dill or basil	50 mL
½ tsp	Tabasco sauce	2 mL
2 tbsp	capers	25 mL
½ tsp	freshly ground pepper	2 mL

1. Remove the skin from the trout. Remove the meat from the bones and flake it into a bowl. You should have approximately 1 lb/500 g.

2. Combine the remaining ingredients and toss with the trout until very well combined. Taste and adjust the seasonings if necessary.

Scallops Provençal

*Scallops are my very favourite shellfish. They are sweet, succulent and tender.
I love both their taste and texture. This recipe reminds me of one I tasted in
Paris and whenever I make it, I think of all the delicious places I visit when
I'm there.*

*I always buy fresh scallops because their texture is usually far superior
to the frozen. And for this recipe I like to use the larger sea scallops rather
than the very small bay ones.*

*This can be served with lots of French bread or it can be combined with
fettuccine for a wonderful pasta dish. Use 1 lb/500 g fettuccine.*

SERVES 6 TO 8

¼ cup	unsalted butter or olive oil, divided	50 mL
3	cloves garlic, finely chopped	3
I	shallot, finely chopped	I
3	tomatoes, peeled, seeded and finely chopped	3
⅓ cup	dry white wine	75 mL
1½ lb	scallops	750 g
¼ cup	chopped fresh parsley	50 mL
	Salt and freshly ground pepper to taste	

1. Melt half the butter in a large skillet and add the garlic and shallots. Cook until very fragrant and tender, but do not brown.

2. Add the tomatoes and wine and cook until the sauce is reduced and somewhat thicker, about 5 minutes.

3. In another skillet, melt the remaining butter and add the scallops. Cover loosely with buttered parchment or waxed paper and cook for 3 to 4 minutes, or until they are barely cooked. Add half the parsley, taste and season with lots of freshly ground pepper and salt.

4. Add the scallops and any juices to the tomato mixture. Serve with the remaining parsley sprinkled on top.

SZECHUAN ORANGE CHICKEN WINGS

This is a great recipe for those who love Szechuan orange chicken. You can serve the wings with rice for a main course, but I like to serve them as a finger-food appetizer.

MAKES APPROX. 2 DOZEN PIECES

2 lb	chicken wings	I kg
MARINADE		
3	cloves garlic, minced	3
4 tsp	minced ginger root	20 mL
3	green onions, minced	3
⅓ cup	hoisin sauce	75 mL
I tbsp	hot Chinese chili paste (or to taste)	15 mL
2 tbsp	frozen orange juice concentrate	25 mL
2 tbsp	grated orange peel	25 mL
3 tbsp	soy sauce	45 mL
3 tbsp	honey	45 mL
½ tsp	oriental sesame oil	2 mL

1. Cut off the wing tips and reserve for making stock. Cut the remaining wings in half.

2. Combine all the ingredients for the marinade. Add the wings to the marinade, place in a clean plastic bag, tie securely and marinate for a few hours in the refrigerator, turning the bag occasionally to make sure the wings are well coated.

3. Preheat the oven to 400°F/200°C. Line a baking dish with parchment paper. Arrange the wings in a single layer. Bake for 20 minutes, brush with the marinade, turn wings, brush other side and bake for 20 to 25 minutes longer. Serve hot or at room temperature.

1. Hold the chicken wing parallel to counter with fleshy side down. Grip the "drumstick" section with your left hand and the middle section with your right hand. Force the joint up and pull down sharply with your right hand, exposing the bone of the drumstick. Separate the drumstick from the middle section.

2. Hold the middle section in your left hand and the wing tip in your right hand. Force the joint up and pull down sharply with your right hand, exposing the two thin bones of the middle section. Separate the wing tip from the middle section.

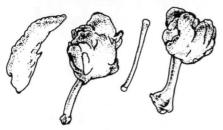

3. Wiggle out the smaller bone from the middle section (it should come free easily). Pull the flesh back from the bone on the middle section and drumstick section, to resemble lollipops. Reserve the wing tips and extra bones and use for stock.

GOAT CHEESE TART WITH OLIVES

This is an irresistible appetizer, but with a salad it can also be served as a main course. It is inspired by a recipe from Joanne Weir, a wonderful California cook who has taught at my school.

SERVES 8

PASTRY

1½ cups	all-purpose flour	375 mL
½ tsp	salt	2 mL
⅔ cup	unsalted butter, cold	150 mL
3 tbsp	ice water, or more if necessary	50 mL

FILLING

4 oz	chèvre (goat cheese)	125 g
4 oz	ricotta cheese	125 g
4 oz	Fontina cheese, chopped or grated	125 g
½ cup	grated Parmesan cheese (preferably Parmigiano Reggiano)	125 mL
½ cup	sour cream or unflavoured yogurt	125 mL
1	clove garlic, minced	1
2 tbsp	chopped fresh rosemary (or 1 tsp/5 mL dried)	25 mL
1 tsp	freshly ground pepper	5 mL
½ tsp	salt	2 mL
½ cup	black olives, pitted and halved	125 mL
1	egg	1
½ tsp	salt	2 mL

1. To make the pastry, combine the flour and salt. Cut in the butter until it is in tiny bits. Sprinkle the water over the mixture and gather the dough into a ball. Add more water if necessary to gather the dough together. Wrap and chill for 30 minutes if you wish.

2. Cream together the chèvre, ricotta, Fontina, Parmesan, sour cream, garlic, rosemary, pepper and ½ tsp/2 mL salt.

3. Preheat the oven to 375°F/190°C.

4. Roll the dough into a 14-inch/35 cm circle. Place on a cookie sheet (without sides) or upside-down jelly-roll pan lined with parchment paper or aluminum foil.

5. Spread the cheese mixture over the dough, leaving a 2-inch/5 cm border. Dot the filling with olives. Fold the border over the cheese (this will leave a flat tart open in the centre).

6. Beat the egg with ½ tsp/2 mL salt and brush over the pastry. Bake for 35 to 40 minutes, or until the crust is brown and the cheese is bubbling and lightly browned. Carefully loosen tart and slide off the pan onto a serving platter. Cool for 10 minutes. Cut into wedges and serve.

VEGETABLES WITH ROUILLE

I am still amazed that people don't use more garlic in cooking, because it is one of the most delicious flavours in the world. When garlic is cooked for a long time, it becomes gentle and sweet-tasting. When it is used raw, it has a much stronger flavour. In this recipe the garlic flavour is rich and vibrant.

This dip can also be used in fish stews for a last-minute burst of flavour, as a sauce for fish or chicken and as a spread for cold meat sandwiches.

SERVES 8 TO 10

1 lb	asparagus	500 g
1	bunch broccoli	1
1 lb	carrots	500 g
8 oz	green beans	250 g
1	large bulb fennel	1
2	Belgian endives	2
½	red cabbage	½

ROUILLE

2	cloves garlic, peeled	2
½	red pepper, roasted and peeled (see page 99)	½
1 cup	mayonnaise	250 mL
¼ tsp	Tabasco sauce	1 mL
1 tsp	Dijon mustard	5 mL
2 tbsp	white wine vinegar	25 mL
½ tsp	salt	2 mL
¼ tsp	freshly ground pepper	1 mL

1. Break the tough ends off the asparagus. Peel a short way up the stalks. Cook the asparagus in boiling water until tender-crisp, about 3 to 5 minutes. Rinse with cold water and pat dry.

2. Trim the tough ends from the broccoli. Cut into pieces so that the florets are on stems for easier dipping. Cook for 2 to 3 minutes until tender-crisp. Rinse with cold water and pat dry.

3. Peel and trim the carrots and cut into 2-inch/5 cm sticks, or cut into carrot flowers as shown. If the carrots are thick, cut them in half. Cook for 3 to 4 minutes until tender-crisp, rinse with cold water and pat dry.

4. Trim the beans. Cook for 2 to 3 minutes until tender-crisp, rinse with cold water and pat dry.

5. Cut the fennel into sticks. Break apart the Belgian endives.

6. Hollow out the red cabbage to use as a container for the dip and use the insides in another recipe.

7. Arrange the vegetables attractively on a large platter.

8. Prepare the rouille by pureeing the garlic and pepper in a blender or food processor.

9. Add the mayonnaise, Tabasco, mustard, vinegar, salt and pepper. Blend for just a second or two or mayonnaise will become too thin. Taste and adjust the seasonings if necessary.

10. Spoon the rouille into the hollowed-out cabbage and place in the centre of the vegetables.

LOWER-FAT VERSION: *Use light mayonnaise or half mayonnaise and half yogurt cheese (see page 28).*

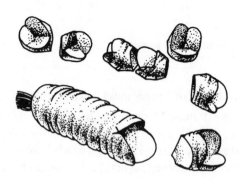

YOGURT CHEESE

Yogurt cheese has been made in the Middle East for centuries, but with the interest in low-fat dairy products it is now becoming popular here, and is even available commercially in some areas.

Yogurt cheese is simply the yogurt solids with the whey drained out to make a thicker, richer mixture. Be sure to use natural yogurt rather than the kind that contains thickeners. You can buy special compact containers made especially to drain the yogurt, but all you really need is a strainer and some cheesecloth or paper towel.

Yogurt cheese can be used in place of sour cream or cream cheese in dips and spreads. It can be used as a garnish in soups or on top of baked potatoes. Use it in place of mayonnaise in sandwich fillings, or instead of mayonnaise or regular yogurt in salad dressings. Or you can mix it with sugar, honey or maple syrup to top desserts.

MAKES 1½ CUPS/375 ML

3 cups	unflavoured natural yogurt (low-fat or regular)	750 mL

1. Line a strainer with cheesecloth, paper towel or a coffee filter. Place over a bowl.

2. Place the yogurt in the strainer. Allow to rest for 3 hours or overnight (the longer it sits, the thicker the yogurt cheese will be). About half the volume of yogurt will drain into the bowl as liquid. Discard the liquid or use it for cooking rice or making bread. Spoon the thickened yogurt cheese into another container. Cover and use as required.

YOGURT CHEESE DIP
Combine 1½ cups/375 mL yogurt cheese with 2 minced cloves garlic, 3 tbsp/50 mL each chopped fresh cilantro, parsley and chives. Add 1 tbsp/15 mL chopped fresh tarragon (or a pinch dried), ½ tsp/2 mL salt, ¼ tsp/1 mL pepper and a dash of Tabasco. Serve with vegetables for dipping.
MAKES ABOUT 1½ CUPS/375 ML.

YOGURT CHEESE DESSERT TOPPING
Combine 1½ cups/375 mL yogurt cheese with 3 tbsp/50 mL granulated sugar, brown sugar, honey or maple syrup. Add 1 tsp/5 mL vanilla extract, 1 to 2 tbsp/15 to 25 mL liqueur or 1 tsp/5 mL grated orange or lemon peel. Taste and adjust seasonings if necessary.
MAKES ABOUT 1½ CUPS/375 ML.

SOUPS

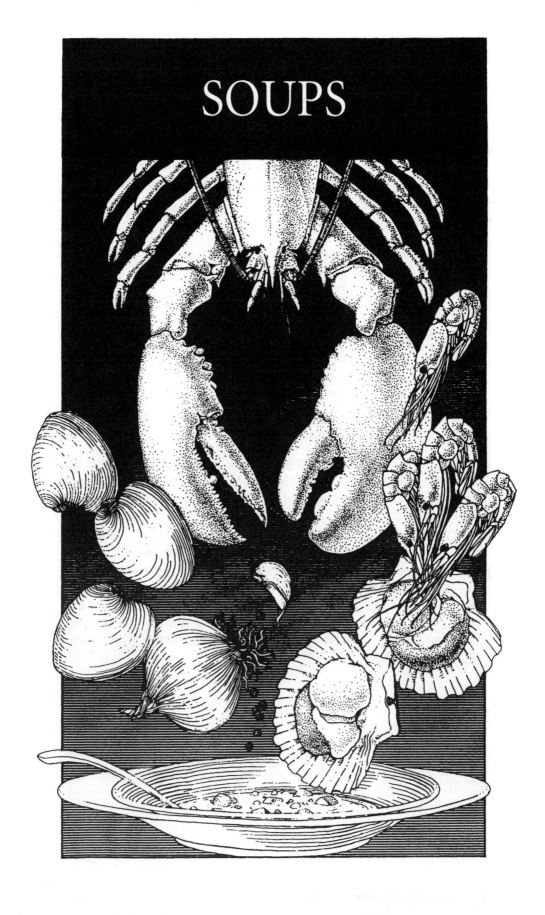

CHICKEN SOUP

Some people believe that the best chicken soup is made with a kosher chicken. I have discovered that you don't necessarily need a kosher chicken, but it is true that the better the chicken, the better the soup will be. If I want to use the chicken soup in recipes that call for chicken stock, then I usually dilute it a bit to get more mileage out of it.

This soup keeps for about one week in the fridge and a few months in the freezer. The boiled chicken can be used in salads, soups or sandwiches, but most of its flavour will be in the stock.

MAKES APPROX. 3 QT/3 L

I	raw chicken, approx. 3 lb/1.5 kg	I
3 qt	cold water (more or less if needed)	3 L
2	carrots, cut into large chunks	2
2	onions, cut into large chunks	2
4	ribs celery, cut into large chunks	4
2	leeks, cut into large chunks (optional)	2
I	parsnip, cut into large chunks (optional)	I
I	parsley root (optional)	I
	Few sprigs fresh parsley	
½ tsp	dried thyme	2 mL
I	bay leaf	I

1. Cut the chicken into small pieces. Place the chicken, bones, skin, etc. (everything except the liver and giblets, as they tend to discolour the soup) in a large stock pot or Dutch oven. Add cold water just to cover. Bring to a boil. Skim off any scum that forms on the surface.

2. Add the carrots, onions, celery, leeks, parsnip and parsley. Add the seasonings and reduce the heat. Allow the soup to simmer gently for 1½ to 2 hours.

3. Strain the soup and place it in the refrigerator overnight. All the fat will rise to the surface and solidify, so that it can be removed easily. However, if you intend to keep the soup for a few days, leave the fat on as a protective cover and use the soup from underneath. If you are going to use the soup right away, the best way to remove the fat is to skim it off with a large spoon. Add salt and pepper to taste as you use the soup.

Scallop and Asparagus Soup

This is an elegant but low-calorie soup with delicate Asian overtones.

Oriental sesame oil is used as a seasoning, not as a cooking oil. Be sure to buy the flavourful, fragrant, dark sesame oil found in Asian food stores and use just a little.

SERVES 6 TO 8

1 tbsp	vegetable oil	15 mL
2	cloves garlic, finely chopped	2
2 tsp	finely chopped fresh ginger root	10 mL
2	leeks, trimmed and sliced	2
4 cups	chicken or fish stock	1 L
1 tbsp	soy sauce	15 mL
½ tsp	oriental sesame oil (optional)	2 mL
8 oz	asparagus	250 g
8 oz	scallops, diced	250 g
3	green onions, sliced	3
	Salt and freshly ground pepper to taste	

1. Heat the oil in a large saucepan and add the garlic, ginger and leeks. Cook for 5 to 10 minutes, without browning, until the vegetables are very fragrant and tender.

2. Add the stock and bring to a boil. Add the soy sauce and sesame oil. Reduce the heat and simmer gently for 20 minutes.

3. Meanwhile, clean the asparagus and trim off the tough stalks. Peel the stalks a few inches up the stems so they will be more tender. Cut the asparagus into approximately 1-inch/2.5 cm pieces. Add to the soup and cook for 5 more minutes. Add the scallops and cook 3 minutes longer.

4. Add the green onions. Taste the soup and season with salt and pepper if necessary. Serve immediately or remove from the heat and reheat very briefly just before serving.

Belgian Endive Soup

Many people are unfamiliar with the slightly sweet, slightly bitter flavour of Belgian endive. It is wonderful in raw salads but is also delicious cooked in this unusual soup.

SERVES 6 TO 8

2 tbsp	unsalted butter or olive oil	25 mL
3	leeks, trimmed and sliced	3
5	Belgian endives, sliced	5
3	potatoes, peeled and diced	3
4 cups	chicken stock	1 L
½ tsp	freshly ground pepper	2 mL
	Salt to taste	
½ cup	cream	125 mL

1. Melt the butter in a large saucepan and add the leeks. Cook until wilted and tender, but do not brown. Add the endives and cook a few minutes longer.

2. Add the potatoes and combine well. Add the stock and pepper and bring to a boil. Cover and cook until tender, about 25 minutes.

3. Puree half the soup in a food processor, blender or food mill, and return to the remaining soup. (If you prefer a completely smooth texture, puree all the soup.) Add the cream and heat thoroughly. Taste and season with salt if necessary.

LOWER-FAT VERSION: *Use only 1 tbsp/15 mL olive oil to cook the leeks. Omit the cream. If the soup is too thick, add additional stock.*

FENNEL AND LEEK SOUP

Fennel has a slightly anise or licorice flavour. Raw, it can be used in salads or served with dips. Cooked, its flavour becomes more gentle but adds a mysterious, subtle taste. Celery can be used if fennel is unavailable but, of course, the flavour will be quite different.

SERVES 8

2 tbsp	unsalted butter or olive oil	25 mL
3	leeks, trimmed and thinly sliced	3
3	bulbs fennel, trimmed (see page 118) and coarsely chopped	3
3 cups	chicken stock	750 mL
I cup	whipping cream or additional chicken stock	250 mL
	Salt and freshly ground pepper to taste	

1. Melt the butter in a large saucepan or soup pot. Add the leeks and cook until soft and tender, but do not allow them to brown.

2. Stir in the fennel and continue to cook for 5 minutes.

3. Add the chicken stock and bring to a boil. Reduce the heat, cover and simmer gently for 30 minutes, or until the vegetables are tender.

4. Puree the soup in a blender, food processor or food mill. Return to the saucepan and stir in the cream. Heat thoroughly and add salt and pepper as necessary.

LOWER-FAT VERSION: *Use 1 tbsp/15 mL olive oil to cook the leeks. Remember to use stock instead of whipping cream.*

CORN SOUP WITH HERB CHEESE

This is a wonderful way to enjoy fresh corn. The cheese melts and the whole thing is heavenly! If you prefer the soup very smooth, pass it through a food mill after cooking.

SERVES 6 TO 8

8	ears corn (or 6 cups/1.5 L frozen niblets)	8
2 tbsp	unsalted butter or olive oil	25 mL
I	onion, chopped	I
I	clove garlic, finely chopped	I
3 cups	milk	750 mL
	Salt and freshly ground pepper to taste	
½ cup	cream	125 mL

GARNISH

6 oz	herbed cream cheese (e.g., Boursin or Rondelé)	175 g
½ cup	chopped fresh parsley or green onions	125 mL

1. Cut the niblets off the ears of corn and process in a blender or food processor. (If you are using a blender, add up to ½ cup/125 mL water to help blend.)

2. Melt the butter in a large saucepan. Cook the onion and garlic for a few minutes. Add the corn and cook for 5 minutes. Do not brown.

3. Add the milk, bring to a boil, cover and reduce the heat. Simmer for 30 minutes (watch closely to prevent burning). Season with salt and pepper to taste.

4. Stir in the cream and adjust the seasonings if necessary. Heat thoroughly.

5. Place 1 oz/30 g cheese in each serving bowl. Spoon in the hot soup and sprinkle with chopped parsley.

   LOWER-FAT VERSION: *Use only 1 tbsp/15 mL olive oil to cook the onion and garlic. Use low-fat milk in place of the regular milk and cream. Use half the amount of herbed cream cheese or use a yogurt cheese dip (see page 28).*

Spinach Soup with Dill and Lemon

Adding rice is a good way to thicken a soup (for people with gluten allergies, this is an especially useful tip). To keep the soup a bright-green colour, do not overcook the spinach and do not cover it while it is cooking.

This soup is also wonderful served hot.

SERVES 6 TO 8

2 tbsp	unsalted butter or olive oil	25 mL
2	onions, finely chopped	2
I lb	spinach, washed well, tough stems removed	500 g
3 tbsp	uncooked rice	45 mL
I	10-oz/282 g package frozen peas	I
3 tbsp	chopped fresh dill	45 mL
4 cups	chicken stock	I L
	Salt, freshly ground pepper and nutmeg to taste	
	Grated peel of ½ lemon	
½ cup	whipping cream	125 mL

GARNISH

½ cup	sour cream	125 mL
8	scallion brushes (see illustration)	8

1. Melt the butter in a large saucepan and cook the onions until tender.

2. Add the spinach and cook, stirring, until it wilts. Add the rice and peas and toss well. Add the dill.

3. Add the chicken stock and just a little salt, pepper and nutmeg. (These seasonings can be adjusted after the soup is chilled and the flavours blend.) Add the lemon peel. Bring to a boil, reduce the heat and simmer for 20 minutes, or until the rice is tender.

4. Puree the soup in a food mill, blender or food processor. Chill.

5. Before serving, stir in the whipping cream. Taste and adjust seasonings.

6. To serve, place a spoonful of sour cream on each serving and float a scallion brush on the sour cream. An alternate garnish is to float paper-thin slices of lemon on the soup.

LOWER-FAT VERSION: *Use 1 tbsp/15 mL olive oil to cook the onions. Omit the whipping cream. Garnish the soup with light sour cream or low-fat yogurt.*

SEAFOOD CHOWDER

This is an elegant, rich soup that can be served as an appetizer, or with homemade bread or rolls for a light lunch or supper.

SERVES 6 TO 8

2 tbsp	unsalted butter or olive oil	25 mL
2	onions, finely chopped	2
I	clove garlic, finely chopped	I
4 cups	milk	I L
	Salt and freshly ground pepper to taste	
½ tsp	dried thyme	2 mL
¼ tsp	hot red chili flakes	I mL
3	potatoes, peeled and diced	3
8 oz	raw shrimp, coarsely chopped	250 g
8 oz	raw scallops, coarsely chopped	250 g
8 oz	raw clams, shucked, or 5-oz/142 g tin baby clams (use the liquid as part of the milk in the recipe)	250 g
8 oz	lobster pieces (if available), or more of any seafood above	250 g

GARNISH

	Chopped fresh parsley or chives	

1. Melt the butter in a large pot and cook the onions and garlic, without browning, until tender.

2. Stir in the milk and gently bring to a boil (the milk can burn easily). Add the salt, pepper, thyme and hot red chili flakes.

3. Add the potatoes and cook gently, covered, for 30 minutes. Puree half the soup and return it to the pot (the pureed potatoes will thicken the soup).

4. Add the seafood and cook for a few minutes, or just until cooked. Taste and adjust the seasonings if necessary. Serve hot, garnished with parsley or chives.

LOWER-FAT VERSION: *Use low-fat milk. Use 1 tbsp/15 mL olive oil to cook the onions and garlic.*

Cold Cream of Tomato Soup with Basil

This soup tastes best when it is made with fresh tomatoes in season. However, you can also use two 28-oz/796 mL tins Italian plum tomatoes, pureed with their juices, and reduce the stock to 1½ cups/375 mL. Omit the tomato paste.

An interesting garnish for this soup is a few sun-dried tomatoes, cut into julienne strips. Sun-dried tomatoes are dried plum tomatoes, usually packed in olive oil. The best ones have an intense but sweet flavour. If fresh basil is not available, use dill. This soup is also delicious served hot.

SERVES 6 TO 8

2 tbsp	olive oil	25 mL
I	clove garlic, finely chopped	I
I	onion, finely chopped	I
I	carrot, finely chopped	I
¼ cup	all-purpose flour	50 mL
2 lb	tomatoes, peeled, seeded and chopped	I kg
2 tbsp	tomato paste	25 mL
I	bay leaf	I
½ tsp	dried thyme	2 mL
3 cups	chicken stock	750 mL
	Salt and freshly ground pepper to taste	
2 tbsp	chopped fresh basil	25 mL
2 tbsp	chopped fresh parsley	25 mL
½ cup	whipping cream	125 mL

GARNISH

I cup	sour cream	250 mL
¼ cup	chopped fresh basil or parsley	50 mL
2	sun-dried tomatoes, cut in julienne	2

1. Heat the oil in a large pot. Cook the garlic, onion and carrot until tender.

2. Stir in the flour and cook carefully for 5 minutes. Do not brown.

3. Stir in the tomatoes, tomato paste, bay leaf, thyme and chicken stock. Add salt and pepper to taste.

4. Bring to a boil, cover, reduce the heat and cook very gently for 30 minutes. Add the basil and parsley and cook for 1 minute.

5. Puree the mixture in a blender or food processor and chill thoroughly.

6. Just before serving, stir in the whipping cream. Taste and reseason with salt and pepper if necessary. Serve with a dollop of sour cream on top of each serving and sprinkle with basil and sun-dried tomatoes.

LOWER-FAT VERSION: *Omit the whipping cream. Use light sour cream or low-fat yogurt in the garnish.*

Gumbo Ya Ya

Louisiana cooking is so delicious. I have had the pleasure of eating this hearty soup many times in New Orleans. Andouille is a smoked hot sausage found in the South, but Kolbassa is a good substitute. The texture of this soup should be slightly thick and chunky. Serve it over rice in large soup bowls. Filé (feelay) powder is made of ground sassafras leaves and is used as a thickening agent. Add it after the cooking is finished, or it will get stringy. Filé has a fairly pronounced "grassy" flavour and can be found in specialty spice shops. It adds a traditional taste but if it is hard to find simply omit it.

SERVES 8

¼ cup	vegetable oil	50 mL
8 oz	Kolbassa or Andouille sausage, sliced	250 g
1 lb	skinless, boneless chicken, diced	500 g
½ cup	all-purpose flour	125 mL
2	onions, chopped	2
4	ribs celery, sliced	4
2	red peppers, halved, seeded and diced	2
2	green peppers, halved, seeded and diced	2
3	cloves garlic, chopped	3
4 cups	beef or chicken stock	1 L
	Salt and freshly ground pepper to taste	
½ tsp	Tabasco sauce	2 mL
½ tsp	cayenne pepper (or to taste)	2 mL
6	green onions, sliced	6
	Filé powder (optional)	
3 cups	cooked rice	750 mL

1. Heat the oil in a Dutch oven. Add the sausage and chicken and cook until slightly browned. Remove and reserve.

2. Discard all but ¼ cup/50 mL fat and heat (you may need additional oil). Whisk in the flour and continue to cook carefully over medium-high heat until the roux is dark brown. Be careful not to burn the roux or to splatter yourself (the roux will be very hot).

3. Add the onions, celery, peppers and garlic. Cook for about 5 minutes, until slightly wilted. Add the stock and heat.

4. Return the sausage and chicken meat to the pot. Season with salt, pepper, Tabasco and cayenne. Cover and cook gently for 20 minutes.

5. Add the green onions and cook for 10 minutes longer. Season to taste (the soup should be quite spicy). After cooking, you can stir in a little filé powder, 1 to 2 tbsp/15 to 25 mL, to help thicken the soup. Do not cook after adding it.

6. Serve over cooked rice.

LOWER-FAT VERSION: *Use only 2 oz/60 g sausage or omit it altogether. Use half the amount of oil.*

Beef and Barley Soup with Wild Mushrooms

This is a hearty, flavourful, cold-weather soup. It becomes thicker the second day. My mother makes this all the time without the wild mushrooms, and it's great. But the wild mushrooms add a very strong, woodsy flavour.

Although you can make this in a smaller quantity, I usually make the full recipe and freeze the soup to use on different occasions.

SERVES 12 TO 16

2 lb	stewing beef (with bones)	1 kg
3 qt	cold water	3 L
1 oz	dried wild mushrooms	30 g
½ cup	pearl barley	125 mL
2	onions, chopped	2
2	ribs celery, sliced	2
2	carrots, chopped	2
1 tsp	salt	5 mL
½ tsp	freshly ground pepper	2 mL
½ tsp	dried thyme	2 mL
1	bay leaf	1
1	clove garlic, minced	1
2 tbsp	chopped fresh parsley	25 mL
1 lb	fresh mushrooms, sliced	500 g
1	28-oz/796 mL tin plum tomatoes, pureed	1

1. Combine the meat, bones and water in a large stock pot and bring to a boil. Skim off any scum that rises to the surface. Reduce the heat and simmer for 1 hour.

2. Soak the dried wild mushrooms in 1 cup/250 mL warm water for 20 minutes. Strain the liquid through a paper towel- or cheesecloth-lined strainer to remove the grit or sand. Wash the mushrooms well and chop.

3. Add the dried mushrooms to the soup with the soaking liquid, barley, onions, celery, carrots and seasonings. Cook for another hour.

4. Add the fresh mushrooms and tomatoes. Cook for 30 minutes. Taste and adjust the seasonings. Thin the soup with a little water if necessary.

SWEET RED PEPPER SOUP

A food mill will strain out the pieces of red pepper skin while it is pureeing the soup. If you do not have a food mill, use a blender or food processor, but either peel the peppers (with a vegetable peeler) before cooking, or strain the soup after pureeing if you want the soup to be smooth and delicate.

This soup can also be made with yellow peppers.

SERVES 6

2 tbsp	unsalted butter or olive oil	25 mL
1	large red onion, chopped	1
2	cloves garlic, chopped	2
¼ tsp	hot red chili flakes	1 mL
8	large red peppers, halved, seeded and cut into chunks	8
2½ cups	chicken stock	625 mL
¼ tsp	freshly ground pepper	1 mL
	Salt to taste	
⅓ cup	whipping cream	75 mL

GARNISH

3 oz	chèvre (goat cheese) or cream cheese	100 g
¼ cup	cream or milk	50 mL
3 tbsp	chopped fresh basil	45 mL

1. Melt the butter in a large saucepan or Dutch oven. Add the onion, garlic and hot chili flakes. Cook for 5 to 8 minutes until tender.

2. Add the red peppers. Combine well and cook for 5 minutes.

3. Add the stock, pepper and salt if necessary. Bring to a boil. Reduce the heat, cover and simmer for 25 minutes.

4. Puree the soup through a food mill and return to the saucepan. Add the cream and heat thoroughly.

5. Blend together the chèvre and cream. Swirl a little of the garnish into each serving and sprinkle with basil.

LOWER-FAT VERSION: *Use 1 tbsp/15 mL olive oil to start the soup. Omit the whipping cream. Use low-fat milk in the garnish and drizzle just a little on each serving.*

SPLIT PEA SOUP WITH SMOKED HAM

It seems so long ago, but I can still remember how thrilled I was when my school was chosen to be the first Canadian cooking school featured in Bon Appetit *magazine. This delicate version of pea soup, enriched with whipping cream, was featured in that article.*

SERVES 8 TO 10

I lb	split green peas	500 g
2 qt	water	2 L
I tbsp	vegetable oil	15 mL
3	onions, chopped	3
2	cloves garlic, finely chopped	2
I	rib celery, chopped	I
2	carrots, chopped	2
4 cups	chicken stock	I L
8 oz	smoked ham in I piece, trimmed (preferably Black Forest)	250 g
¼ cup	chopped fresh parsley	50 mL
½ cup	whipping cream	125 mL
	Salt and freshly ground pepper to taste	

GARNISH

4 oz	thinly sliced smoked ham (preferably Black Forest), cut into julienne	125 g

1. Soak the peas in the water for 1 hour.

2. Heat the oil in a heavy, large saucepan over medium-low heat. Add the onions and garlic and cook until translucent, stirring occasionally, about 10 minutes. Add the celery and carrots and cook for 5 minutes.

3. Drain the peas and rinse. Add them to the pan.

4. Stir in the stock and bring to a boil.

5. Stir in the 8-oz/250 g piece of ham and parsley. Reduce the heat, cover and simmer until the peas are very tender, about 1½ hours.

6. Remove the ham from the soup. Taste the ham and reserve if it is still flavourful. Puree the soup in batches in a food processor or blender. Return to the saucepan and thin with chicken stock or water if necessary.

7. Cut the reserved ham into ½-inch/1 cm cubes and return to the soup if desired. Stir in the cream and heat through. Season with salt and pepper.

8. Ladle the soup into bowls. Garnish with the julienned ham and serve. (The soup can be prepared four days ahead. Cover and refrigerate. Thin with chicken stock or water if necessary before serving.)

LOWER-FAT VERSION: *Omit the whipping cream. Reduce the amount of ham or omit it entirely.*

PASTA E FAGIOLI

This is a gusty Italian soup that can be served as an entire meal with crusty bread and a salad. One of my students once left this soup simmering on the stove while she went out shopping for a few hours. When she returned home, the pasta had thickened the soup so much that it had turned into a casserole. Instead of panicking, she poured it into a casserole dish, sprinkled the cheese on top and baked it.

SERVES 8

I tbsp	olive oil	15 mL
2	onions, chopped	2
3	cloves garlic, finely chopped	3
I	carrot, finely chopped	I
8 oz	boneless pork loin, diced	250 g
¼ tsp	hot red chili flakes	I mL
3 cups	chicken or beef stock	750 mL
I	28-oz/796 mL tin plum tomatoes	I
I	19-oz/540 g tin cannellini beans	I
8 oz	pasta, in smallish pieces	250 g
	Salt and freshly ground pepper to taste	
½ cup	grated Parmesan cheese (preferably Parmigiano Reggiano)	125 mL

1. Heat the oil in a large saucepan or Dutch oven and cook the onions, garlic and carrot until fragrant. Add the diced pork and chili flakes and cook until the pork is coloured.

2. Add the stock and tomatoes with their juices (break them up slightly) and bring to a boil. Lower the heat, cover and simmer gently for 30 minutes.

3. Rinse the beans under cold water and add to the soup. Cook for 10 minutes.

4. Puree half the soup and return the pureed soup to the pot.

5. Bring the soup to the boil again and add the pasta. Stir to make sure it does not stick on the bottom and cook for 10 minutes, stirring occasionally. If the soup is too thick, add water to thin it.

6. Taste and season with salt and pepper if necessary. Serve sprinkled with Parmesan cheese.

MAIN COURSES

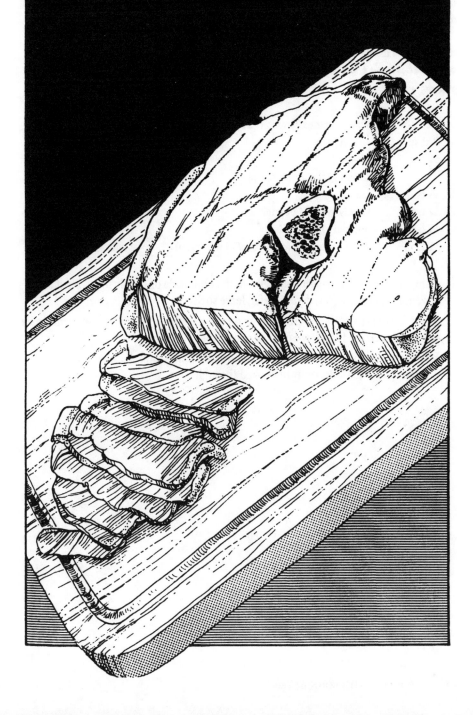

GRILLED TIGER SHRIMP

Many people tell me that they're afraid to have me over for dinner. But like a lot of people in the food business, I am always thrilled to be invited to someone's home. Rather than being critical, most food people are so aware of the time and energy it takes to entertain that they are the most appreciative guests you can find.

One of my students, Irene Tam, took the plunge once and did invite me for dinner. The meal was excellent, and these shrimps, served with fresh asparagus, made up just one of the many courses. Irene claims that I taught her everything she knows about cooking, but if I did, she really added her own wonderful style to it all! Now we invite each other over all the time.

Tiger shrimps are quite large—2 to 3 oz/60 to 90 g each—and quite expensive. However, this recipe can also be made with smaller shrimps, and in this case I usually cook them on skewers.

SERVES 4

12	Tiger shrimps (approx. 2 lb/1 kg)	12
3 tbsp	lemon juice	45 mL
¼ cup	olive oil	50 mL
2	cloves garlic, finely chopped	2
½ tsp	salt	2 mL
¼ tsp	freshly ground pepper	1 mL
¼ tsp	hot red chili flakes	1 mL
¼ tsp	dried rosemary (or 1 tbsp/15 mL fresh)	1 mL

1. Using scissors, cut through the shells on the underside of the shrimps. Shell and devein the shrimps. (Or, if you prefer, leave shells on.)

2. Combine the remaining ingredients and pour over the shrimps. Allow to marinate in the refrigerator for a few hours or overnight.

3. When ready to cook, preheat the broiler or barbecue. Cook the shrimps for 3 to 4 minutes on each side, or until cooked through.

STEAMED SALMON AND GINGER WITH BLACK BEAN SAUCE

Fermented black beans should be stored in the refrigerator after opening. Don't confuse them with dried black turtle beans used in chilis, soups and salads. Fermented black beans are used as a seasoning in Asian dishes and are used in small quantities (a few tablespoons or less). If you can't find them, use 1 tbsp/15 mL black bean sauce (Lee Kum Kee is the best brand).

SERVES 4

4	salmon steaks or fillets (approx. 6 oz/175 g each)	4
2	slices fresh ginger root, coarsely chopped	2
1 tbsp	rice wine	15 mL
1 tsp	salt	5 mL
1 tbsp	vegetable oil	15 mL
1 tbsp	fermented black beans, washed, drained and minced	15 mL
2	cloves garlic, chopped	2
1	green onion, chopped	1
1 tsp	finely chopped fresh ginger root	5 mL
¼ cup	chicken stock or water	50 mL
1 tbsp	soy sauce	15 mL
1 tbsp	rice wine	15 mL

1. Rinse the salmon steaks and pat them dry. Place in a bowl.

2. Combine the ginger slices, 1 tbsp/15 mL rice wine and salt and sprinkle on the salmon. Allow to marinate for 15 minutes. Discard the ginger and place the salmon in a single layer in a flat ovenproof dish.

3. Heat the oil in a wok or skillet and add the beans, garlic, green onion and chopped ginger. Stir-fry until very fragrant (about 10 seconds) and then add the stock, soy sauce and 1 tbsp/15 mL rice wine. Cook for 2 minutes, stirring constantly. Pour the sauce over the fish.

4. Place a steamer rack (or four criss-crossed chopsticks, as shown) in the bottom of the wok. Fill to the bottom of the rack with water. Heat until boiling. Place the dish of fish on the rack and cover. Steam over high heat for 10 to 15 minutes, or just until the fish is cooked. If the water in the wok evaporates too quickly, add some boiling water. Serve immediately. (If you do not have a wok, cover an ovenproof baking dish with foil and bake in the oven at 400°F/200°C for 10 to 15 minutes.)

STIR-FRIED SCALLOPS WITH BROCCOLI

When I went to Taiwan to take cooking classes, I was dismayed to learn that in most restaurants, the meat and sometimes even the vegetables in stir-fried dishes are deep-fried first. However, this doesn't have to be the case in home-style Chinese dishes.

Not only is this recipe quick and delicious—it's also low in calories. Serve it with steamed rice.

SERVES 6

1½ lb	fresh scallops	750 g
2	slices fresh ginger root, smashed	2
2	green onions, smashed	2
2 tbsp	rice wine	25 mL
1	bunch broccoli, trimmed, with the tough skin removed (about 1 lb/500 g)	1
1 tbsp	vegetable oil	15 mL
12	1-inch/2.5 cm pieces green onion	12
1 tsp	finely chopped fresh ginger root	5 mL
2	cloves garlic, finely chopped	2

SAUCE

½ cup	chicken stock	125 mL
1 tsp	salt	5 mL
2 tbsp	rice wine	25 mL
½ tsp	granulated sugar	2 mL
½ tsp	oriental sesame oil	2 mL
2 tsp	cornstarch	10 mL
2 tsp	chopped fresh cilantro	25 mL

1. Rinse the scallops and drain them well. Slice each in half horizontally and place in a bowl.

2. Add the smashed ginger root and green onions to 2 tbsp/25 mL rice wine (this allows the flavours to go into the wine). Combine the scallops with the wine. Toss lightly and allow them to marinate for 30 minutes. Discard the ginger and onions.

3. Meanwhile, slice the broccoli stems on the diagonal. Separate the florets. Cook the broccoli in boiling water for 3 minutes. Refresh under cold water to stop the cooking and set the colour. Pat dry and reserve.

4. Combine all the ingredients for the sauce.

5. Heat a wok or a large skillet. Add the oil. Heat the oil until very hot and add the pieces of green onion, chopped ginger root and garlic. Stir-fry until fragrant.

6. Add the broccoli and sauce to the wok and toss well. Add the scallops. When the sauce has thickened and the scallops are just cooked, about 2 minutes, remove to a platter. Sprinkle with cilantro.

SOLE WITH LEMON AND CAPERS

This lightly battered fish dish is fast and easy to prepare. It's so delicious that it's sure to make fish a family favourite. It also works well with salmon fillets or any thin fillet—it's even great with thin veal or turkey scallops.

SERVES 4

4	sole fillets (approx. 4 oz/125 g each)	4
	Salt and freshly ground pepper	
2	eggs	2
½ cup	all-purpose flour	125 mL
3 tbsp	unsalted butter or olive oil	45 mL
⅓ cup	lemon juice	75 mL
2 tbsp	capers	25 mL
¼ tsp	freshly ground pepper	1 mL
¼ cup	chopped fresh parsley	50 mL

1. Pat the fish dry with paper towels and season lightly with salt and pepper. Place the eggs in a flat dish and beat them together.

2. Dip the fillets into the flour and shake off the excess. Dip the floured fish into the eggs to coat. Redip the fish into the flour.

3. Heat the butter in a large skillet and cook the fish for about 3 minutes on each side (cook in two batches if necessary). Remove to a serving platter and keep warm while preparing the sauce.

4. Discard any excess fat that remains in the skillet. Return the skillet to the heat and add the lemon juice and capers. Deglaze the pan by scraping up any bits of solidified juices and combining them into the sauce. Remove from the heat and add the pepper and the parsley. Pour over the fish and serve immediately.

LOWER-FAT VERSION: *Cook the fish in a non-stick pan and use only 1 to 2 tbsp/15 to 25 mL olive oil. Use 2 egg whites instead of whole eggs.*

LEMON SALMON TERIYAKI

Students over the years have told me that this is one of their favourite recipes. This is a special treat during barbecue season, but it also works beautifully under the broiler or in one of those ridged grill pans you use on top of the stove. Sauce can be made in large quantities and refrigerated or frozen.

SERVES 6

½ cup	soy sauce	125 mL
⅓ cup	granulated sugar	75 mL
¼ cup	rice wine	50 mL
I	clove garlic, minced	I
I tsp	minced fresh ginger root	5 mL
	Juice of I lemon	
I tsp	dry mustard	5 mL
6	salmon steaks or fillets (approx. 6 oz/175 g each)	6

1. Combine all the ingredients except the salmon steaks and bring to a boil. Cook for a few minutes until syrupy.

2. Barbecue or broil the salmon steaks (about 5 minutes on each side if steaks are about 1 inch/2.5 cm thick). Brush with the glaze a few times on each side during cooking.

Whisky-glazed Steak

You can also rub this paste into a 1½-lb/750 g sirloin. Barbecue or broil for 5 to 6 minutes per side and then slice thinly on the diagonal.

SERVES 4

1 tbsp	Worcestershire sauce	15 mL
½ tsp	Tabasco sauce	2 mL
3 tbsp	dry mustard	45 mL
2 tbsp	whisky (or more)	25 mL
4	steaks (New York sirloins, filets or rib—approx. 6–8 oz/175–250 g each)	4

1. Make a paste with the Worcestershire sauce, Tabasco sauce, mustard and whisky. Add more whisky or mustard if needed, but the paste should be pretty thick.

2. Smear the paste all over the steaks and allow to marinate at room temperature for 30 minutes.

3. Barbecue or broil the steaks for 3 to 4 minutes per side (to cook steaks 1 inch/2.5 cm thick medium-rare).

Marinated Flank Steak

Flank steak is very lean, and it is the least expensive cut for grilling. When it is marinated, cooked rare and sliced very thin, it is delicious!

SERVES 4 TO 6

⅓ cup	white wine vinegar	75 mL
⅓ cup	balsamic vinegar	75 mL
2 tbsp	olive oil	25 mL
1	clove garlic, minced	1
2 tbsp	Dijon mustard	25 mL
1 tbsp	Worcestershire sauce	15 mL
¼ tsp	freshly ground pepper	1 mL
1	bay leaf	1
½ tsp	dried thyme	2 mL
1	flank steak (approx. 1 lb/500 g)	1

1. Combine all the ingredients except for the steak. Place in a plastic bag and add the steak. Massage the marinade into the steak and press out any air in the bag. Tie securely. Place in the refrigerator and marinate the meat 8 hours to overnight.

2. Heat the barbecue or broiler.

3. Remove the meat from the marinade and pat dry. Place on the hot grill and cook for 3 to 4 minutes per side for rare. Slice very thinly, on the diagonal.

Steaks with Green Peppercorn Sauce

Green peppercorns are unripe peppercorn berries, and they are much milder than traditional black or white peppercorns (they are available in specialty stores). This sauce also works well with veal chops.

SERVES 4

4	New York sirloins or filets (approx. 6 oz/175 g each)	4
1 tbsp	vegetable oil	15 mL
⅔ cup	dry white or red wine	150 mL
3 tbsp	Cognac	45 mL
½ tsp	Dijon mustard	2 mL
2 tbsp	crushed green peppercorns	25 mL
½ cup	whipping cream	125 mL
2 tbsp	chopped fresh parsley	25 mL

1. Preheat the oven to 200°F/90°C.

2. Dry the steaks well with paper towels. Heat the oil in a heavy skillet and cook the steaks until they are a little less done than you want them in the end. (A steak that is 1 inch/2.5 cm thick will require approximately 3 to 4 minutes on each side for medium-rare.)

3. Remove the steaks to a serving platter and keep them warm in the oven. Discard any excess fat from the pan and return the pan to the heat.

4. Add the wine to the pan and deglaze by scraping the bits of solidified juices off the bottom of the pan and into the sauce. Add the Cognac. Cook until the liquid is reduced by half and slightly thickened.

5. Add the mustard and peppercorns and cook for a few minutes longer. Press the peppercorns with the back of a spoon. Stir in the cream. Bring to a boil and reduce until slightly thickened.

6. Pour the sauce over the steaks and sprinkle with parsley.

LOWER-FAT VERSION: *Use beef or chicken stock, or pureed tomatoes instead of whipping cream.*

Steaks with Mustard Cream Sauce

Add 2 chopped shallots to the pan with the wine. Omit the Cognac and peppercorns. Reduce and stir in 1 tbsp/15 mL Dijon mustard, ½ cup/125 mL whipping cream or pureed tomatoes, ½ tsp/2 mL Worcestershire sauce and salt and pepper to taste. Cook until slightly thickened. Pour the sauce over the steaks and sprinkle with parsley.

BLACKENED SIRLOIN STEAK

This Cajun-style dish is hot, spicy and wonderful. Many different kinds of peppers are used in this mix, but they all add their own particular flavour. Because the spice mix creates a lot of smoke when cooking, it is best to prepare this outdoors on a barbecue or in a kitchen with excellent ventilation.

SERVES 8

1 tbsp	freshly ground white pepper	15 mL
1 tbsp	freshly ground black pepper	15 mL
1 tbsp	salt	15 mL
1 tbsp	dry mustard	15 mL
1 tbsp	paprika	15 mL
2 tsp	cayenne pepper	10 mL
¼ tsp	dried ground fennel (optional)	1 mL
½ tsp	dried thyme	2 mL
½ tsp	dried oregano	2 mL
2 tbsp	unsalted butter or olive oil	25 mL
2	cloves garlic, minced	2
2½ lb	sirloin steak (approx. 1½ inches/4 cm thick)	1.5 kg

1. Combine all the dry spices for the seasoning mix.
2. Melt the butter and combine with the garlic.
3. When you are ready to cook the steak, brush with garlic butter and then pat the seasonings into each side.
4. Preheat the barbecue and barbecue the steak for 5 to 7 minutes on each side for rare, depending on the thickness of the steak. The steak will blacken, so do not worry. Also, a lot of smoke will be created by the seasoning mix. Douse the flames with water if necessary.

Mustard-glazed Sirloin Steak

Barbecued sirloin steak, carved into thin slices on the diagonal, reminds me of a mini roast, where every slice has a great barbecue flavour. If it is not barbecue season, broil it or use a ridged grill pan on top of the stove.

SERVES 8

I	2-lb/I kg sirloin steak (approx. I ½ inches/4 cm thick)	I
⅓ cup	Dijon mustard	75 mL
2 tbsp	lemon juice	25 mL
I tbsp	Worcestershire sauce	15 mL
½ tsp	Tabasco sauce	2 mL
½ tsp	freshly ground pepper	2 mL
I tbsp	soy sauce	15 mL

1. Pat the steak dry.

2. Combine the remaining ingredients and spread the mixture on both sides of the steak. Allow to marinate in the refrigerator for 30 minutes, or up to 3 hours.

3. Preheat the barbecue or broiler or grill pan. Cook the steak for 6 to 8 minutes per side for medium-rare. Allow the steak to rest for 5 minutes before carving. Slice on the diagonal.

BARBECUED BRISKET

This barbecued brisket is actually baked in the oven, with a hot, spicy, barbecue sauce. It is easy to prepare but should bake for a long time so that the meat becomes very tender. I prefer a double brisket because it is juicier, but it does contain more fat. To make this mild, use 1 tsp/15 mL mustard, omit the Tabasco sauce and tin of chopped green chilies.

SERVES 6 TO 8

I	5-lb/2.5 kg brisket	I
3	onions, sliced	3
I cup	ketchup	250 mL
½ cup	chili sauce	125 mL
I cup	water	250 mL
I	4-oz/110 g tin chopped green chiles	I
¼ cup	Dijon mustard	50 mL
2 tbsp	vinegar	25 mL
I tbsp	Worcestershire sauce	15 mL
I tsp	Tabasco sauce	5 mL
½ tsp	freshly ground pepper	2 mL
2	cloves garlic, minced	2

1. Preheat the oven to 350°F/180°C.
2. Pat the brisket dry. Place the onions in the bottom of a roasting pan and sit the brisket on top.
3. Combine the remaining ingredients and pour over the top of the meat.
4. Cover tightly and roast for 3½ hours. Every hour, remove the lid and add additional water if the pan is getting dry. There should always be at least 1 cup/250 mL liquid in the bottom of the pan.
5. After 3½ hours, remove the lid and return to the oven for 20 to 30 minutes until brown.

Spicy Burgers

For juicy, delicious hamburgers, try these.

Hamburgers will all cook at the same time (even if they are different weights) if they are the same thickness. Be sure to cook hamburgers thoroughly.

SERVES 8

2 lb	lean ground beef	1 kg
½ cup	hot taco sauce (use mild if you wish)	125 mL
1	egg	1
2	cloves garlic, minced	2
1 tsp	chili powder	5 mL
1	small onion, finely chopped	1
½ cup	fresh breadcrumbs	125 mL
	Salt and freshly ground pepper to taste	

1. Combine all the ingredients together well. Shape into eight patties.

2. Barbecue or pan fry for about 8 minutes on each side for medium. Turn them carefully.

Braised Short Ribs in Barbecue Sauce

Braised dishes are coming back into favour as they are easy to make and don't require constant attention. Because they take a while to cook, I always make lots and freeze the leftovers for another time. Short ribs are an inexpensive cut of meat, but when they are cooked properly, they are tender and full of flavour.

Serve these ribs with mashed potatoes.

SERVES 8

8	short ribs, approx. 3 inches/7.5 cm each (about 4 lb/2 kg)	8
I tbsp	paprika	15 mL
I tbsp	chili powder	15 mL
I tsp	ground cumin	5 mL
I tsp	dry mustard	5 mL
I tsp	freshly ground pepper	5 mL
I tsp	salt	5 mL
SAUCE		
I tbsp	vegetable oil	15 mL
3	onions, sliced	3
4	cloves garlic, finely chopped	4
¾ cup	ketchup	175 mL
¾ cup	chili sauce	175 mL
I cup	beer, beef stock or water	250 mL
I tbsp	pureed chipotle chiles (see page 120)	15 mL
3 tbsp	Worcestershire sauce	45 mL
2 tbsp	Dijon mustard	25 mL

1. Trim the excess fat from the ribs. Combine the spices and dust on the ribs. Marinate up to overnight in the refrigerator.

2. Heat the oil in a Dutch oven or braising pan that can be used on top of the stove and in the oven. Brown the ribs well. Remove from the pan.

3. Preheat the oven to 350°F/180°C.

4. Discard the excess fat from the pan and add the onions and garlic. Cook for a few minutes. Add the remaining sauce ingredients and stir well. Add the short ribs. Bring to a boil.

5. Cover and bake for 2½ hours, or until the ribs are very tender.

6. Remove the ribs to a serving dish. Skim the fat from the sauce and taste and adjust the seasonings if necessary. Pour the sauce over the ribs.

Deviled Chicken

This is a simple presentation, so start with a really good-quality chicken. You can make it more "devilish" by adding more Tabasco, pepper and chili flakes. The chicken can also be broiled.

SERVES 4

2 tbsp	olive oil	25 mL
¼ cup	lemon juice	50 mL
2 tbsp	Dijon mustard	25 mL
I tsp	Tabasco sauce	5 mL
½ tsp	salt	2 mL
½ tsp	freshly ground pepper	2 mL
½ tsp	dried rosemary (or I tbsp/15 mL fresh)	2 mL
¼ tsp	hot red chili flakes	I mL
I	chicken, cut into serving pieces (approx. 4 lb/2 kg)	I

1. Combine the oil, lemon juice, mustard, Tabasco sauce, salt, pepper, rosemary and chili flakes. Taste and correct seasonings.

2. Rub the mixture into the chicken and allow it to marinate for 30 minutes.

3. Preheat the barbecue and barbecue the chicken skin side down for 10 minutes. Then turn and cook for 15 to 20 minutes, until the juices run yellow when the chicken is pierced. Baste with extra marinade during the cooking.

LOWER-FAT VERSION: *Use skinless chicken breasts with bone in (to keep them juicier). Reduce oil to 1 tbsp/15 mL. Do not overcook.*

APRICOT-GLAZED CHICKEN

This flavourful recipe is fast and easy, but it makes a dinner taste very special. The chicken is perfect served hot, but is also great cold for picnics.

SERVES 4 TO 6

1	chicken (approx. 4 lb/2 kg)	1
½ cup	apricot jam	125 mL
2 tbsp	Dijon mustard	25 mL
2 tbsp	soy sauce	25 mL
1 tsp	Worcestershire sauce	5 mL
½ tsp	Tabasco sauce	2 mL
1	clove garlic, minced	1
1 tsp	minced fresh ginger root	5 mL

1. Preheat the oven to 375°F/190°C.

2. Cut the chicken into 4 or 6 pieces. Pat dry. Place the chicken skin side up on a jelly-roll pan lined with aluminum foil or parchment paper.

3. Combine the remaining ingredients in a small saucepan and cook until well blended, about 2 to 3 minutes.

4. Brush the glaze on the chicken. Bake for 40 to 50 minutes, or until the chicken is just cooked through. Baste occasionally.

   LOWER-FAT VERSION: *Use skinless chicken breasts, bone in, and cook for only 30 to 35 minutes, or until just cooked through.*

CHICKEN WITH RASPBERRY VINEGAR

This is stunning in appearance and flavour. It is also easy and quick to prepare and low in calories. In short—perfect!

You can use sherry vinegar or balsamic vinegar instead of the raspberry vinegar. You can also use your favourite herb, fresh or dried, instead of rosemary.

Serve this with a rice pilaf (see page 107).

SERVES 6

1½ lb	boneless, skinless chicken breasts	750 g
	All-purpose flour	
3 tbsp	unsalted butter or olive oil	50 mL
	Salt and freshly ground pepper to taste	
½ tsp	dried rosemary (or 2 tbsp/25 mL fresh)	2 mL
⅓ cup	raspberry vinegar	75 mL
4 oz	snow peas	125 g
1 lb	cherry tomatoes	500 g

1. Preheat the oven to 200°F/90°C.

2. Cut the chicken into 1½-inch/4 cm pieces.

3. Shake the chicken strips with flour in a large sieve over a bowl (so that the excess flour gets sifted away).

4. In a wok or large non-stick skillet, heat half the butter or oil. Add the chicken pieces and cook, stirring constantly, until cooked through. This should not take too long as the pieces are small and breast meat is very tender. While the chicken is cooking, season with salt, pepper and rosemary. (You may have to cook the chicken in two batches.)

5. Remove the chicken to a serving platter and keep warm in the oven.

6. Discard any fat left in the skillet and return to medium heat. Add the vinegar and cook until it is reduced to a few tablespoons. Scrape the bottom of the pan to remove any bits of chicken (this deglazing will add a lot of flavour to the sauce). Pour the sauce over the chicken.

7. Return the pan to the heat and add the remaining butter or oil. Add the snow peas and cook for 2 minutes. Add the cherry tomatoes and cook just until heated through. Season with salt and pepper. Arrange the vegetables around the chicken.

Voodoo Chicken with Cornbread Stuffing

*Cajun cooking became so popular that people have blackened everything.
I think I have even heard of a blackened cheesecake! This lightly blackened
chicken breast is superb. It is best to barbecue the chicken outdoors, because
it smokes a lot, but do not overcook it—the outside should be spicy and crisp
and the inside should be juicy and tender. Be sure to serve it with the
cornbread stuffing.*

SERVES 6

CORNBREAD STUFFING

2 tbsp	unsalted butter or olive oil	25 mL
2	red onions, chopped	2
3	cloves garlic, finely chopped	3
2	ribs celery, chopped	2
2	red peppers, peeled, seeded and chopped	2
I	green pepper, peeled, seeded and chopped	I
I	4-oz/110 g tin chopped green chiles	I
I tsp	chili powder	5 mL
½ tsp	salt (or more to taste)	2 mL
¼ tsp	freshly ground black pepper	I mL
¼ tsp	freshly ground white pepper	I mL
4 cups	diced cornbread (see page 124)	I L
2	eggs, lightly beaten	2
½ cup	sour cream or yogurt	125 mL

VOODOO CHICKEN

3	large whole chicken breasts, split and boned but with the skin left on (each boned piece of chicken should weigh about 5 oz/150 g)	3
2 tbsp	unsalted butter, melted, or olive oil	25 mL
3	cloves garlic, minced	3
2 tsp	freshly ground black pepper	10 mL
2 tsp	freshly ground white pepper	10 mL
2 tsp	paprika	10 mL
½ tsp	cayenne pepper	2 mL
I tsp	dry mustard	5 mL
¼ tsp	dried thyme	I mL
¼ tsp	dried oregano	I mL
I	small piece bay leaf, crushed	I
I tsp	salt	5 mL

1. To prepare the stuffing, heat the butter or oil in a large skillet and add the onions and garlic. Cook until tender and fragrant.

2. Add the celery, peppers and chiles. Cook for a few minutes until the vegetables are very tender. Season with chili powder, salt, black and white pepper and toss with the cornbread. Taste and adjust seasonings if necessary.

3. Stir in the eggs and sour cream or yogurt. If you are cooking the stuffing on the barbecue, brush a large piece of foil with butter, place the stuffing in the centre and wrap to form a tight package. Barbecue for about 20 minutes per side. (If you are oven-baking the stuffing, place in a buttered 3-qt/3 L casserole dish and bake at 375°F/190°C for 30 to 40 minutes, or until the top is browned.)

4. To prepare the chicken, pat the chicken breasts dry. Combine the melted butter or oil and garlic and place in a flat dish. Dip pieces of chicken in the garlic-butter mixture so that both sides are coated. Allow to marinate until ready to cook.

5. Combine all the remaining ingredients. Just before cooking, sprinkle this spice mixture evenly over both sides of the chicken and pat in slightly.

6. Barbecue the chicken for approximately 5 to 7 minutes per side, skin side first, until barely cooked. Or place the chicken in a baking dish and bake at 375°F/190°C for 35 to 40 minutes. (The chicken won't be as blackened, but it will still be good.)

LOWER-FAT VERSION: *In the stuffing, use 1 tbsp/15 mL olive oil to cook the onions and garlic, and cook over low heat. Use 4 egg whites instead of 2 whole eggs. Use low-fat yogurt instead of sour cream. Remove skin from chicken and use olive oil in step 4.*

CHINESE EMERALD CHICKEN

This is also good made with turkey breast or pork tenderloin. Serve it with rice for a complete meal.

SERVES 6

2 tbsp	vegetable oil	25 mL
1 lb	boneless, skinless chicken breasts, cut into chunks	500 g
1 tbsp	finely chopped fresh ginger root	15 mL
1	onion, sliced	1
1	green pepper, seeded and diced	1
½ lb	broccoli, cut into 1 inch/2.5 cm chunks	250 g
2	ribs celery, sliced	2
4 oz	snow peas	125 g
	Salt and freshly ground pepper	
½ cup	chicken stock	125 mL
2 tbsp	soy sauce	25 mL
1 tbsp	rice wine	15 mL
1 tbsp	cornstarch	15 mL
¼ cup	water	50 mL
1 tbsp	sesame seeds, toasted	15 mL

1. Heat the oil in a wok.

2. Dry the chicken pieces well and add to the wok with the ginger. Stir and cook until the chicken whitens.

3. Stir in the onion and cook for a few minutes. Add the remaining vegetables and cook for a few minutes longer. Season with salt and pepper.

4. Add the stock, soy sauce and wine. Cover and cook until the liquid comes to a boil. Cook for 2 minutes. Reduce the heat and cook gently for 2 to 3 minutes.

5. Combine the cornstarch with the water and stir until smooth. Increase the heat. Mix into vegetables and cook until just thickened. Sprinkle with sesame seeds.

Smoked Chicken Hash

This is a great way to use up leftover cooked fish, chicken, turkey and, of course, corned beef. For a treat, try putting a poached or fried egg on top—the yolk breaks into a luscious sauce for the hash.

SERVES 4

1 tbsp	olive oil	15 mL
2	strips bacon, diced	2
1	onion, chopped	1
2	cloves garlic, finely chopped	2
2 cups	diced smoked chicken or leftover roast chicken (approx. 1 lb/500 g)	500 mL
2 cups	diced boiled potatoes (approx. 1 lb/500 g)	500 mL
	Salt and freshly ground pepper to taste	
3	green onions, chopped	3
¼ cup	whipping cream	50 mL

1. Heat the oil in a large skillet. Add the bacon and cook until crisp.

2. Add the onion and garlic. Cook until tender. Add the chicken and potatoes and cook for a few minutes. Add the salt, pepper and green onions.

3. Mash the mixture slightly and stir in the cream. Cook until a bit crusty and browned.

LOWER-FAT VERSION: *Omit the bacon. Use chicken stock instead of whipping cream.*

MARMALADE-GLAZED LEG OF LAMB

Whenever I think of the birth of my daughter, Anna, I think of this leg of lamb. I was cooking it just as I had the first suspicion of labour. My doctor husband, Ray, wouldn't let me eat any of it, just in case. He was right, of course, as Anna was born just two hours later, but it was the first barbecue of the season and the lamb was pink and juicy and smelled just wonderful. I really was craving some. When my good friends Jim and Carol White heard this story, they were sympathetic. As parents of two children themselves, Jenny and Jason, they knew I had probably received enough flowers and baby sleepers. So they sent me a leg of lamb! It was the most thoughtful and original present ever given to a new mother.

SERVES 6

I	leg of lamb, butterflied (approx. 4 lb/2 kg after boning)	I
I tbsp	olive oil	15 mL
I tsp	salt	5 mL
GLAZE		
½ cup	marmalade	125 mL
I tbsp	minced fresh ginger root	15 mL
I	clove garlic, minced	I
¼ cup	Dijon mustard	50 mL
2 tbsp	soy sauce	25 mL
I tsp	Worcestershire sauce	5 mL
½ tsp	Tabasco sauce	2 mL

1. Pat the lamb dry and flatten out as much as possible. Remove any excess fat. Brush lightly with the oil. Sprinkle with salt.

2. Preheat the barbecue or broiler.

3. Combine the ingredients for the glaze and heat.

4. Cook the lamb 15 minutes per side for rare. Brush with the glaze a few times during cooking. Allow the lamb to rest for 5 to 10 minutes before carving. Slice thinly.

LEMON MINT LAMB CHOPS

Compound butters were once a chef's secret. But they are so easy to prepare, look so good and taste so terrific that they are a trick well worth learning. Even a very thin slice looks and tastes great. They can be made with a multitude of seasonings and served on any plain cooked meat or fish.

This recipe will make more butter than you need; freeze any extra for another occasion.

SERVES 4

8	loin lamb chops	8
3 tbsp	lemon juice	45 mL
½ tsp	salt	2 mL
2 tbsp	olive oil	25 mL
I tbsp	chopped fresh mint (or ½ tsp/2 mL dried)	15 mL

LEMON MINT BUTTER

½ cup	unsalted butter, at room temperature	125 mL
2 tbsp	lemon juice	25 mL
I tbsp	chopped fresh mint (or ½ tsp/2 mL dried)	15 mL
	Salt and freshly ground pepper to taste	

1. Trim excess fat off the lamb chops. Combine the lemon juice, salt, olive oil, mint and pepper. Marinate the lamb in this mixture in a flat dish, turning often, for at least 30 minutes at room temperature or longer in the refrigerator.

2. While lamb is marinating, prepare the compound butter. Cream the butter with the lemon juice, mint and salt and pepper to taste. Place the butter on a piece of waxed paper and shape into a cylinder about 3 x 1½ inches/7.5 x 4 cm. Refrigerate.

3. Broil, barbecue or pan fry the lamb chops approximately 3 to 5 minutes on each side (they should be slightly rare). Slice the butter thinly and place two slices on each hot chop. The butter will melt slowly and moisten and flavour the lamb.

LOWER-FAT VERSION: *Use only a very thin slice of the lemon butter, or omit it entirely.*

BRAISED LAMB SHANKS

Lamb shanks are a tough cut of meat, but they become meltingly tender when they are cooked for a long, slow time. Tough cuts of meat have more flavour than tender cuts, and they are so reasonable in price, they are well worth exploring.

Serve this over mashed potatoes, rice, polenta or pureed beans.

SERVES 8 TO 12

8	lamb shanks (approx. 10–12 oz/300–375 g each)	8
2 tbsp	olive oil	25 mL
3	onions, sliced	3
6	cloves garlic, finely chopped	6
¼ tsp	hot red chili flakes	1 mL
2	carrots, chopped	2
1	28-oz/796 mL tin plum tomatoes, chopped or pureed, with juices	1
1 cup	dry white wine	250 mL
1 cup	chicken stock or beef stock	250 mL
1 tbsp	chopped fresh rosemary (or ½ tsp/2 mL dried)	15 mL
1 tbsp	chopped fresh thyme (or ½ tsp/2 mL dried)	15 mL
1 tsp	salt	5 mL
½ tsp	freshly ground pepper	2 mL
½ cup	chopped fresh parsley	125 mL

1. Trim the lamb shanks. Heat the olive oil in a Dutch oven and brown the lamb well, a few shanks at a time if necessary. Remove and reserve.

2. Preheat the oven to 350°F/180°C.

3. Discard all but a few tablespoons of oil from the Dutch oven. Add the onions and garlic and cook until tender and fragrant, about 8 minutes. Add the chili flakes and carrots. Cook for 5 minutes.

4. Add the tomatoes, wine, stock, rosemary, thyme, salt and pepper. Bring to a boil.

5. Return the lamb to the Dutch oven. Cover and bake for 2 to 3 hours, or until very, very tender.

6. If necessary, defat the sauce. If the sauce is too liquidy, remove the shanks and keep warm. Cook the sauce, uncovered, over medium-high heat, until it reduces to the consistency you wish. Season to taste.

7. Serve each guest a whole lamb shank or cool slightly and remove the meat from the bones, return it to the sauce, heat thoroughly, and serve like a stew. Sprinkle with parsley before serving.

PROVIMI VEAL LIVER

Provimi liver is the most delicate and the most expensive, but this dish is also great with calves' liver. Along with barbecued liver, this is one of my favourite preparations.

SERVES 4 TO 6

1½ lb	Provimi veal liver, sliced ½ inch/1 cm thick	750 g
1 cup	all-purpose flour	250 mL
2	eggs	2
3 cups	fresh breadcrumbs	750 mL
2 tbsp	crushed black peppercorns	25 mL
1 tsp	salt	5 mL
¼ cup	unsalted butter	50 mL

GARNISH

	Thin lemon slices	

1. Remove any skin from the liver. If necessary, cut into serving pieces. (Sometimes the liver is cut in long slices, which would be too much for one serving. Each serving should be 4 to 5 oz/125 to 150 g.)

2. Have on hand a plate of flour, another plate with the beaten eggs in it and another plate of breadcrumbs combined with the peppercorns and salt. Pat the liver dry with paper towels and then dust with flour. Dip into the egg to coat well and then into the crumbs. Pat the crumbs into the liver firmly and set on a rack to dry. Refrigerate until ready to cook.

3. In a large, heavy skillet, melt the butter. Cook the liver on medium heat for 4 to 5 minutes on each side. The crumbs should be crisp but not too brown, and the liver should be medium-rare. Garnish with lemon slices.

VEAL SCALOPPINE WITH MARSALA CREAM SAUCE

Although all Marsala wine is "sweet," when you cook with it, be sure to use the driest version you can find. This recipe also works beautifully with veal chops, chicken breasts or turkey scallops.

SERVES 3 TO 4

2 tbsp	unsalted butter or olive oil	25 mL
1 lb	thin veal scallops	500 g
½ cup	all-purpose flour	125 mL
½ cup	dry Marsala	125 mL
⅓ cup	whipping cream	75 mL
	Salt and freshly ground pepper to taste	

1. Heat the butter in a large skillet.

2. Dredge the scallops in the flour and add to the pan (you may have to do this in two batches).

3. Brown the scallops quickly (a minute or so on each side). When they are brown, transfer them to a platter and keep warm.

4. Pour off any fat remaining in the pan and return to the heat. Add the Marsala.

5. Scrape the bottom of the pan, stir, and add the cream. Stir constantly over high heat until the sauce thickens a little. Season with salt and pepper to taste. Pour the sauce over the scallops.

LOWER-FAT VERSION: *Use chicken stock instead of whipping cream. Use olive oil to cook the veal.*

Western Barbecued Pork Chops

This is a great way to have pork chops. Tender chops can be used, but butt chops, which are often less tender and less expensive, work especially well— they become moist and juicy when marinated and cooked this way.

If there is extra marinade and you want to use it as a sauce, cook the marinade for 5 to 10 minutes, uncovered, until it thickens and the raw juices are thoroughly cooked. If you do not like a very spicy sauce, cut down on the Tabasco, hot chili flakes, mustard and banana pepper.

SERVES 6 TO 8

3 lb	butt pork chops (approx. 1½ lb/750 g each)	1.5 kg

MARINADE		
1½ cups	barbecue sauce or ketchup	375 mL
1 tbsp	Worcestershire sauce	25 mL
1 tsp	Tabasco sauce	5 mL
¼ tsp	hot red chili flakes	1 mL
2 tbsp	Dijon mustard	25 mL
¼ cup	honey	50 mL
¼ cup	lemon juice or vinegar	50 mL
2	onions, finely chopped	2
3	cloves garlic, minced	3
1	banana pepper, chopped	1
½ cup	ketchup	125 mL

1. Place the pork chops in a large plastic bag.

2. Combine all the ingredients for the marinade and pour into the bag with the chops. Seal. Marinate in the refrigerator overnight.

3. Prepare the barbecue. When the coals are covered with a grey ash, barbecue the chops. If they are approximately 1 inch/2.5 cm thick, they will take 15 to 20 minutes on each side. Baste with the marinade as they cook. Be careful, as they can burn easily. These can also be baked in the sauce at 375°F/190°C for about 1 hour, or until the meat is very tender.

SWEET AND SOUR SPARERIBS

When I took cooking lessons in Tai-pei, I learned to deep-fry ribs before braising them. But since I rarely deep-fry at home, I was pleased that these came out so well when I omitted this step. You could broil or stir-fry the ribs first, if you wish, or precook them in broth or water for 10 minutes.

SERVES 4 TO 6

3 lb	spareribs, split down the centre lengthwise by the butcher	1.5 kg
1	piece fresh ginger root, smashed	1
2	green onions, cut in large pieces and smashed	2
2 tsp	rice wine	10 mL
1½ tsp	soy sauce	7 mL
2 tbsp	vegetable oil	25 mL
1 tsp	finely chopped fresh ginger root	5 mL
1 tbsp	finely chopped garlic	15 mL
½ cup	ketchup	125 mL
4 cups	chicken stock or water	1 L
¼ cup	granulated sugar	50 mL
1 tsp	salt	5 mL
1½ tsp	rice vinegar	7 mL
1 tsp	oriental sesame oil	5 mL

1. Cut the ribs into individual pieces.

2. Combine the smashed ginger, smashed green onions, 2 tsp/10 mL rice wine and soy sauce. Place in a bowl with the ribs and toss well. Allow to marinate for at least 30 minutes. Discard the ginger and green onions and pat the ribs dry.

3. Heat the oil in a wok. Add the chopped ginger and garlic and cook until fragrant.

4. Add the ketchup, chicken stock, sugar, salt and 1½ tsp/7 mL vinegar. Bring to a boil and add the ribs to the wok.

5. Cover the pan and cook the ribs on medium-high heat for approximately 30 minutes. Remove the cover and cook on high heat, stirring constantly, until the ribs are well glazed and almost all the liquid has evaporated (this may take 10 to 15 minutes).

6. Sprinkle the ribs with the sesame oil and serve immediately.

CHINESE BARBECUED RIBS

I have always thought the secret of tender barbecued ribs is to precook them. That way they lose some of their fat, and they do not dry out or burn from sugary sauces when they are barbecued.

SERVES 6

4 lb	back or side ribs	2 kg
½ cup	ketchup	125 mL
½ cup	hoisin sauce	125 mL
3	cloves garlic, minced	3
1 tbsp	minced fresh ginger root	15 mL
1 tbsp	hot Chinese chili paste	15 mL
3 tbsp	soy sauce	45 mL
1 tsp	oriental sesame oil (optional)	5 mL
1 tbsp	Dijon mustard	15 mL
2 tbsp	honey	25 mL

1. Cut the racks of ribs in half. Cook the ribs in simmering water for 45 minutes. Drain and cool.

2. Combine the remaining ingredients. Marinate the ribs in the refrigerator for 1 hour or overnight.

3. Barbecue for 10 to 15 minutes per side (or bake for 10 to 15 minutes per side at 400°F/200°C). Brush with any excess marinade during the cooking.

CHINESE-STYLE BARBECUED PORK

This can be served hot or cold as a main course or as an appetizer. The sauce can also be used over chicken or turkey breasts. Five-spice powder is actually a combination of six spices—fennel seed, anise, ginger, licorice root, cinnamon and cloves! You can buy it pre-mixed.

SERVES 4 TO 6

2 tbsp	hoisin sauce	25 mL
1 tbsp	oyster sauce	15 mL
2 tbsp	soy sauce	25 mL
1 tbsp	rice wine	15 mL
1 tbsp	hot Chinese chili paste	15 mL
3 tbsp	honey	45 mL
1 tsp	salt	5 mL
¼ tsp	freshly ground pepper	1 mL
½ tsp	five-spice powder (optional)	2 mL
2	cloves garlic, minced	2
1 tbsp	minced fresh ginger root	15 mL
2 lb	pork tenderloin or centre cut boneless pork loin, cut into pieces lengthwise, about 2 inches/5 cm thick	1 kg

1. Combine all the ingredients except for the pork.

2. Place the pieces of pork and the marinade in a plastic bag and marinate for 1 hour or overnight in the refrigerator.

3. Barbecue or roast at 350°F/180°C for 30 to 45 minutes, turning frequently. (If you are using a meat thermometer, the meat should register 160°F/70°C when done.)

PASTAS AND
LIGHT MEALS

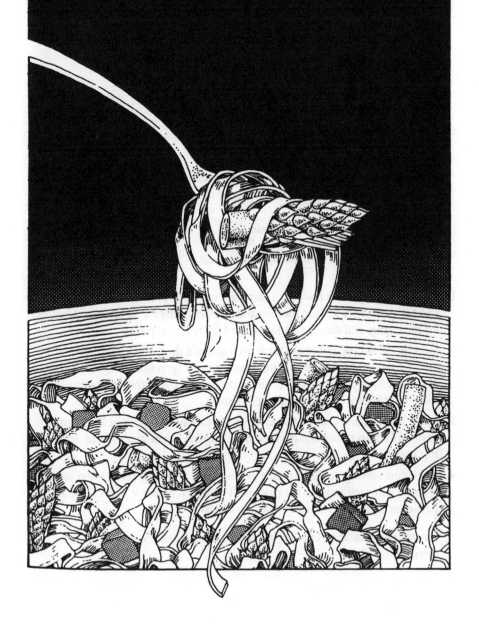

Penne with Mixed Sausages and Red Peppers

This recipe was a result of a delicious trip to the St. Lawrence Market in Toronto. The array of homemade sausages along with the peppers and tomatoes was an inspiration.

Penne are the noodles that look like pen nibs, but you can use rigatoni instead.

SERVES 6 TO 8

2	hot Italian sausages (approx. 3 oz/90 g each)	2
2	sweet Italian sausages (approx. 3 oz/90 g each)	2
2 tbsp	olive oil	25 mL
3	cloves garlic, finely chopped	3
1/4 tsp	hot red chili flakes	1 mL
1	red onion, chopped	1
3	red peppers, peeled and cut into 2-inch/5 cm chunks	3
3	tomatoes, peeled, seeded and chopped	3
	Salt and freshly ground pepper to taste	
1 lb	penne	500 g
1/2 cup	grated Parmesan cheese (preferably Parmigiano Reggiano)	125 mL
2 tbsp	chopped fresh parsley and/or basil	25 mL

1. Prick the sausages in a few places and place in a deep skillet. Cover with cold water and bring to a boil. Reduce the heat and simmer gently for 30 minutes. Cool, peel off the casings and slice the sausages into 1-inch/2.5 cm pieces.

2. Heat the oil in deep skillet or Dutch oven and add the garlic, chili flakes and onion. Cook over medium heat until tender and fragrant but do not brown. Add the red peppers and cook until the peppers wilt. Add the cooked sausage slices and tomatoes. Cook for about 5 minutes.

3. Add a little salt and pepper. Cook, stirring occasionally, for about 20 minutes. Taste and adjust seasonings if necessary. (The dish can be made ahead up to this point.)

4. Just before serving, cook the penne in a large pot of boiling salted water until tender. Drain well and toss the pasta with the sauce. Sprinkle with cheese and parsley or basil. Toss well and serve immediately.

LOWER-FAT VERSION: *Use half the sausages and half the olive oil.*

Fettuccine with Smoked Chicken and Hazelnuts

To toast hazelnuts, spread the nuts on a baking sheet and bake at 350°F/180°C for 5 to 10 minutes, or until toasted. Gather the nuts in a tea towel and rub together until the skins flake off. You will not be able to rub off all the skins, but don't worry.

SERVES 4 TO 6

2 tbsp	unsalted butter	15 mL
2	shallots or garlic, finely chopped	2
¾ cup	whipping cream	175 mL
2 cups	diced smoked chicken meat	500 mL
	Salt and freshly ground pepper to taste	
8 oz	chèvre (goat cheese)	250 g
½ cup	finely chopped toasted hazelnuts	125 mL
¼ cup	grated Parmesan cheese (preferably Parmigiano Reggiano)	50 mL
I lb	fettuccine	500 g
2 tbsp	chopped fresh parsley	25 mL

1. Melt the butter in a large skillet, cook shallots or garlic gently for 2 to 3 minutes, add the cream. Bring to a boil.

2. Add the chicken and cook until the chicken is heated through. Season lightly with salt and pepper. Keep warm.

3. In a large serving bowl, break the chèvre into small pieces. Sprinkle with the nuts and Parmesan cheese.

4. Just before serving, cook the fettuccine in a large pot of boiling salted water. Cook until tender but still slightly firm. Drain well.

5. Add the fettuccine to the cheese and nuts. Pour the hot chicken-cream mixture on top. Toss well. Taste and adjust seasonings if necessary. Sprinkle with parsley.

LOWER-FAT VERSION: *Use olive oil instead of butter. Use pureed tomatoes instead of whipping cream.*

Linguine with Smoked Salmon and Lemon Sauce

This is my version of one of the most popular restaurant pasta dishes of all time. Rich and luxurious in taste, calories and price, it was everyone's favourite including mine. It was introduced to Toronto by Raffaello Ferreri who was one of Toronto's most talented young chefs.

This is great as an appetizer. Or you can leave out the smoked salmon and serve it with a main course such as roast chicken or lamb. You could also substitute smoked ham for the salmon.

SERVES 6 AS AN APPETIZER

2 tbsp	unsalted butter	25 mL
2	cloves garlic, finely chopped	2
¾ cup	whipping cream	175 mL
1 tsp	grated lemon peel	5 mL
8 oz	smoked salmon, diced	250 g
1 lb	linguine	500 g
2 tbsp	lemon juice	25 mL
2 tbsp	vodka	25 mL
½ cup	grated Parmesan cheese (preferably Parmigiano Reggiano)	125 mL
	Salt, freshly ground pepper and nutmeg to taste	
2 tbsp	chopped fresh dill or green onions	25 mL

1. Heat the butter in a large skillet and cook the garlic until fragrant and tender but not brown. Add the cream and lemon peel and boil gently until slightly thickened, about 5 minutes. Add the smoked salmon and cook just until heated through.

2. Meanwhile, add the linguine to a large pot of boiling salted water. Cook just until tender.

3. Drain the linguine well and toss with the cream mixture, lemon juice, vodka and cheese. Toss until the cream clings to the pasta and thickens. Season with salt, pepper and nutmeg. Sprinkle with fresh dill.

ORIENTAL PESTO WITH NOODLES

I first tasted this unusual version of pesto in San Francisco at the home of my friend Loni Kuhn. We met when we attended Marcella Hazan's classes in Italy and have been fast friends ever since. One of the nice things about taking cooking classes is the people you meet, not just what you learn. Loni is a fabulous cook and cooking teacher and has introduced me to many wonderful dishes, including this one.

Basically there are three different types of parsley—the regular curly-leaf parsley, the flat-leaf Italian parsley, and cilantro, sometimes known as fresh coriander or Chinese parsley. The first two types are similar and can be used interchangeably. But cilantro has quite a different taste altogether. It is usually available in Chinese markets (ask for Chinese parsley) or in West Indian and Mexican markets (cilantro) or East Indian markets (call it fresh coriander). It may seem to be hard to find, but you have to call it by its right name at the right store. If you really can't find it, or if you don't like it, just use more parsley.

SERVES 6 TO 8

½ cup	peanut oil	125 mL
I cup	unsalted peanuts	250 mL
4	cloves garlic, peeled	4
I	I-inch/2.5 cm piece fresh ginger root, peeled	I
2	banana peppers, seeded and ribbed	2
¼ tsp	hot red chili flakes (optional)	I mL
½ cup	packed fresh basil leaves	125 mL
½ cup	packed fresh mint leaves	125 mL
½ cup	packed fresh parsley	125 mL
½ cup	packed fresh cilantro	125 mL
I tsp	salt (or more to taste)	5 mL
¼ cup	lemon juice	50 mL
I½ lb	fettuccine or linguine	750 g

1. Heat the oil in a skillet and brown the peanuts carefully. Do not allow them to burn. Drain on paper towels and cool.

2. In a food processor fitted with the steel knife, chop the garlic and ginger into a paste. Add the peppers and chop. Add the nuts and chop.

3. Add the chili flakes and herbs and chop until very fine and the mixture is well blended.

4. Add the salt and the lemon juice and taste. Adjust the seasonings if necessary. Reserve until ready to serve.

5. Add the noodles to a large pot of boiling salted water and cook until tender. Stir about ¼ cup/50 mL of the boiling water into the pesto to warm it. Drain the pasta and shake out the excess water. Toss with the sauce and serve immediately.

Fettuccine with Ham and Asparagus

In the spring when the first asparagus appears on the market, this makes a wonderful appetizer or Easter brunch dish. It is as beautiful as it is flavourful.

If the pasta has been freshly made, it should take only a minute to cook. Store-bought "fresh" pasta usually takes 5 to 6 minutes, and commercial dried pasta usually takes 10 to 12 minutes.

SERVES 4 AS AN APPETIZER

1 lb	fresh asparagus	500 g
2 tbsp	unsalted butter	25 mL
1	clove garlic, finely chopped	1
½ cup	chicken stock or water	125 mL
½ cup	whipping cream	125 mL
4 oz	cooked ham, diced	125 g
	Salt and freshly ground pepper to taste	
1 tsp	Russian-style mustard (such as Honeycup)	5 mL
pinch	cayenne pepper	pinch
1 lb	fettuccine	500 g
3 tbsp	chopped fresh dill	45 mL
½ cup	grated Parmesan cheese (preferably Parmigiano Reggiano)	125 mL

1. Trim off the tough bases of the asparagus and discard. Peel the stems only if they are tough. Dice in 1 inch/2.5 cm pieces.

2. Heat the butter in a skillet and add the garlic and diced asparagus. Cook until fragrant.

3. Add the chicken stock and cook until reduced to a few tablespoons. Add the cream and ham and cook until the sauce has reduced and thickened slightly. Season lightly with salt and pepper and stir in the mustard and cayenne.

4. Bring a large pot of salted water to a boil. When the sauce is ready, add the pasta to the water and cook until tender.

5. Drain the pasta well and place it in a large, flat bowl. Add the dill, cheese and sauce and toss well. Taste and adjust seasonings if necessary.

LOWER-FAT VERSION: *Use olive oil instead of the butter. Use pureed tomatoes instead of whipping cream. Omit the mustard. Use half the cheese.*

SPAGHETTI WITH SEAFOOD SAUCE

The inspiration for this recipe came after taking Marcella Hazan's cooking course in Bologna.

This is a great way to make a pound of expensive seafood go a long way. Serve small portions as an appetizer or serve with a salad as a main course.

To toast fresh breadcrumbs, place them in a dry skillet and shake the pan over medium heat until the breadcrumbs are crisp and brown. Or spread the breadcrumbs on a baking sheet and toast at 350°F/180°C until brown, about 5 to 7 minutes. Watch them carefully.

SERVES 4 TO 6

¼ cup	olive oil	50 mL
3	cloves garlic, finely chopped	3
¼ tsp	hot red chili flakes	1 mL
¼ cup	chopped fresh parsley or basil	50 mL
8 oz	scallops, chopped	250 g
8 oz	shrimp, shelled, deveined and chopped	250 g
1 lb	spaghetti	500 g
⅓ cup	toasted fresh breadcrumbs	75 mL
	Salt and freshly ground pepper	

1. Heat the oil in a large skillet. Add the garlic and chili flakes and cook until fragrant but do not brown.

2. Add half the parsley and all the seafood. Cook for 2 to 3 minutes. Remove from heat.

3. Cook the spaghetti in a large pot of boiling salted water until tender. Drain well and toss with the sauce, breadcrumbs and remaining parsley. Season with salt and pepper to taste and serve immediately.

PENNE WITH CREAMY SAUSAGE SAUCE

I remember having a dish similar to this at a restaurant in Bologna. I dreamed about it for five years but for some reason never thought to make it. One night when I was having dinner at one of my favourite Italian restaurants, Mastro's, the owners, Rina and Livio Camaro, served me something very close to it. So I went back to my kitchen and came up with this.

SERVES 6 TO 8

I tbsp	olive oil	15 mL
3	cloves garlic, finely chopped	3
¼ tsp	hot red chili flakes (optional)	I mL
12 oz	sweet Italian sausages, removed from casings and crumbled	375 g
¾ cup	whipping cream	175 mL
I tsp	salt	5 mL
¼ tsp	freshly ground pepper	I mL
¼ tsp	nutmeg	I mL
I lb	penne	500 g
½ cup	grated Parmesan cheese (preferably Parmigiano Reggiano)	125 mL
2 tbsp	chopped fresh parsley or basil	25 mL

1. Heat the oil in a large skillet. Add the garlic, hot red chili flakes and crumbled sausage meat. Cook until all traces of pink disappear, about 5 minutes.

2. Add the whipping cream, salt, pepper and nutmeg and bring to a boil. Reduce the heat and simmer gently for about 10 minutes, or until the cream reduces and sauce thickens somewhat.

3. Meanwhile, cook the pasta in a large pot of boiling salted water. Drain the noodles well but do not rinse.

4. Toss the noodles with the sauce, cheese and parsley. Taste and adjust seasonings if necessary.

LOWER-FAT VERSION: *Use one 28-oz/796 mL tin plum tomatoes, drained and pureed, instead of the cream.*

Bugialli's Fresh Tomato Sauce with Spaghetti

It is hard to believe something this easy could be so good. It's one of my favourite recipes from Giuliano Bugialli, popular Italian cooking teacher. Giuliano comes to Toronto every year and delights my students with his tales of Italian history, music and literature. He's a true Renaissance man.

SERVES 4 TO 6

2 lb	ripe tomatoes	1 kg
¼ cup	olive oil	50 mL
1	small tin anchovy fillets (about 8), minced	1
2	cloves garlic, minced	2
¼ tsp	hot red chili flakes (or more to taste)	1 mL
	Salt and freshly ground pepper to taste	
1 lb	spaghetti	500 g
	Chopped fresh parsley	

1. Preheat the oven to 400°F/200°C.

2. Slice the tomatoes and arrange in large baking dish. (It doesn't matter if the tomatoes are layered.) Add the olive oil and sprinkle with anchovies, garlic, chili flakes, salt and pepper.

3. Bake for 30 to 40 minutes, or until the tomatoes are tender and break up when touched with a wooden spoon.

4. Cook the spaghetti for 10 to 12 minutes. Drain well (do not rinse) and add to the tomatoes. Toss gently. To serve, sprinkle with parsley.

MACARONI AND CHEESE

You just can't beat good macaroni and cheese. The unusual twist to this version is curry powder—it does not dominate, but rather adds a subtle, mysterious flavour.

SERVES 6 TO 8

½ lb	macaroni	250 g
¼ cup	unsalted butter	50 mL
¼ cup	all-purpose flour	50 mL
4 cups	milk, hot	1 L
1 tbsp	Dijon mustard	15 mL
1 tsp	curry powder	5 mL
1 tsp	salt	5 mL
¼ tsp	freshly ground pepper	1 mL
1 tsp	Worcestershire sauce	5 mL
¼ tsp	Tabasco sauce	1 mL
¼ tsp	nutmeg	1 mL
3 cups	grated Cheddar cheese	750 mL

TOPPING

1 cup	fresh breadcrumbs	250 mL
½ cup	grated Cheddar cheese	125 mL
¼ cup	unsalted butter, melted	50 mL

1. Preheat the oven to 350°F/180°C.

2. Bring a large pot of salted water to a boil. Cook the macaroni until tender; do not overcook. Drain in a colander and rinse with cold water. Reserve.

3. While the macaroni is cooking, prepare the sauce. Melt ¼ cup/50 mL butter in a saucepan and add the flour. Cook on low heat and stir for about 5 minutes.

4. Whisk in the hot milk and bring to a boil. Reduce the heat and add seasonings.

5. Add 3 cups/750 mL cheese and cook gently for 5 minutes more, or until the cheese melts. Taste again and adjust seasonings.

6. Combine the sauce with the macaroni and place in a buttered 13- x 9-inch/3 L casserole dish.

7. Combine all the topping ingredients and spread over the top. Bake for 30 minutes, or until the sauce bubbles and the top browns.

LOWER-FAT VERSION: *Use half the butter in the sauce and topping. Use low-fat milk. Use extra old or old cheddar and use only half the cheese.*

Fettuccine California Style

Chèvre, or goat cheese, has always been popular in Europe. But it wasn't until they started making excellent goat cheese in California, and California chefs and food writers started to promote it, that it became so popular all across North America.

This creamy, luscious sauce works well with white or green pasta. I like to use a mild, creamy-style Canadian goat cheese.

SERVES 6 TO 8

2 tbsp	unsalted butter	25 mL
1	clove garlic, finely chopped	1
1 cup	whipping cream	250 mL
6 oz	chèvre (goat cheese)	175 g
1 tsp	chopped fresh rosemary (or ¼ tsp/1 mL dried)	5 mL
1 tsp	chopped fresh thyme (or ¼ tsp/1 mL dried)	5 mL
1 tbsp	chopped fresh basil or parsley	15 mL
1 tsp	salt	5 mL
½ tsp	freshly ground pepper	2 mL
1 lb	white or green fettuccine	500 g
¼ cup	grated Parmesan cheese (preferably Parmigiano Reggiano)	50 mL

1. To make the sauce, melt the butter in a skillet. Add the garlic and cook gently, without browning, until fragrant. Add the cream and bring to a boil. Cook until the liquid reduces and thickens slightly.

2. Whisk the goat cheese into the cream until smooth. Add the herbs, salt and pepper.

3. Cook the pasta in a large pot of boiling salted water until tender. Drain well. Toss with the sauce and Parmesan cheese. Taste and adjust seasonings if necessary.

LOWER-FAT VERSION: *Eat less!*

SPAGHETTINI WITH SUN-DRIED TOMATOES

This is great to serve as a light meal or as an appetizer. All kinds of wonderful ingredients like wild mushrooms, sun-dried tomatoes and fresh herbs make this dish spectacular.

Spaghettini is thin spaghetti. Of course, if you can't find it, use spaghetti instead.

SERVES 6 TO 8

I oz	dried wild mushrooms (approx.)	30 g
¾ cup	warm water	175 mL
¼ cup	olive oil	50 mL
3	cloves garlic, finely chopped	3
¼ tsp	hot red chili flakes	I mL
¼ cup	sun-dried tomatoes, cut into strips	50 mL
4 oz	fresh mushrooms (wild or regular), sliced	125 g
½ cup	black olives, pitted and cut into large pieces	125 mL
I tsp	salt	5 mL
¼ tsp	freshly ground pepper	I mL
I lb	spaghettini	500 g
¼ cup	chopped fresh basil or parsley	50 mL

1. Place the dried mushrooms in the warm water and allow them to soak for 30 minutes. Drain the mushrooms, reserving the liquid. Wash the mushrooms to get rid of any sand or dirt and cut them into strips. Reserve. Strain the soaking liquid through a coffee filter or paper towels and reserve.

2. Heat the olive oil in a large skillet and add the garlic and chili flakes. Cook, without browning, until very fragrant.

3. Add the tomatoes, fresh mushrooms, dried mushrooms and the soaking liquid. Cook until the liquid in the pan has almost evaporated.

4. Add the olives, salt and pepper. Remove from the heat.

5. Cook the pasta in a large pot of boiling salted water. Drain well. Reheat the sauce just before the pasta is ready. Toss the pasta with the sauce and basil. Taste and adjust seasonings if necessary.

LOWER-FAT VERSION: *Use half the amount of olive oil and half the olives.*

Spaghetti with Pesto Sauce

This is an all-time favourite summer recipe. The sauce can also be frozen for a fresh taste of basil all year round, and it keeps for about two weeks in the refrigerator. It can also be stirred into rice or mashed potatoes, or it can be used as a pizza topping. And it is wonderful served as a condiment with lamb.

Nuts are relatively expensive and high in fat, but toasting them really increases their flavour, so you can use less. Place the nuts on a baking sheet and bake at 350°F/180°C for 5 to 7 minutes, or until brown.

Only fresh herbs must be used in this recipe.

SERVES 8 TO 10 AS AN APPETIZER

3	cloves garlic, peeled	3
½ cup	pine nuts, toasted	125 mL
1 cup	packed fresh parsley leaves	250 mL
2 cups	packed fresh basil leaves	500 mL
½ cup	grated Parmesan cheese (preferably Parmigiano Reggiano)	125 mL
½ cup	olive oil	125 mL
1 tsp	salt	5 mL
¼ tsp	freshly ground pepper	1 mL
1½ lb	spaghetti	750 g
¼ cup	unsalted butter	50 mL

1. Place the garlic in a food processor or blender and process until finely chopped. Add the nuts and chop until very fine. (If you are not using a blender or food processor, chop finely with a knife or use a mortar and pestle.)

2. Chop the parsley and basil and add to the garlic-nut mixture. Blend in the cheese.

3. Slowly beat in the olive oil—the mixture should be thick. Season with salt and pepper. (The dish can be made ahead to this point.)

4. Cook the spaghetti in a large pot of boiling salted water.

5. Just before the spaghetti is ready, add ¼ cup/50 mL boiling spaghetti water to the pesto sauce to warm it gently. Drain the spaghetti and toss with the butter and sauce.

LOWER-FAT VERSION: *Use half the amount of pine nuts, cheese and olive oil. Omit the butter. If the mixture is dry, add tomato juice.*

Spaghetti with Garlic and Oil

This simple sauce is one of the most delicious (sometimes using only a few ingredients in a dish has greater impact than using many).

SERVES 6

½ cup	olive oil	125 mL
4	cloves garlic, finely chopped	4
¼ tsp	hot red chili flakes	1 mL
¼ cup	dry breadcrumbs	50 mL
¼ cup	chopped fresh parsley	50 mL
1 tsp	salt	5 mL
¼ tsp	freshly ground pepper	1 mL
1 lb	spaghetti	500 g

1. Heat the oil in a large, deep skillet. Add the garlic and hot chili flakes and cook gently until very fragrant. Add the breadcrumbs, parsley, salt and pepper.

2. Meanwhile, cook the spaghetti in a large pot of boiling salted water.

3. Drain the spaghetti and add to the sauce. Toss on low heat. Taste and adjust the seasonings if necessary.

BOW TIES WITH ASPARAGUS AND GORGONZOLA CREAM

Rhonda Caplan, who works with me at the cooking school, devised this recipe for a quick dinner for her husband, Fred Struzer. Although she is lactose intolerant and couldn't eat any, he made up for it by having four helpings. That was her first clue that the recipe was a big success.

This is rich, so I like to serve it as an appetizer in small quantities, but I guess you could also use up a whole day's fat calories in one meal, as Fred did!

SERVES 4 TO 6

1 lb	fresh asparagus	500 g
½ cup	whipping cream	125 mL
4 oz	Gorgonzola cheese	125 g
	Salt and freshly ground pepper to taste	
1 tbsp	chopped fresh tarragon (or ½ tsp/2 mL dried)	15 mL
¾ lb	bow ties or other pasta	375 g

1. Trim the asparagus and peel about 1 inch/2.5 cm up the stems. Cook in a skillet filled with simmering water until barely tender. Drain, rinse with cold water and pat dry. Cut into 1-inch/2.5 cm pieces.

2. Heat the cream in a large, deep skillet and crumble in the Gorgonzola. Allow to melt. Add the salt, pepper and tarragon. Remove from the heat.

3. Before serving, cook the pasta in a large pot of boiling salted water. Reheat the sauce gently and add the asparagus. Drain the pasta well and add to the sauce. Toss on low heat and serve.

THAI CHICKEN AND NOODLE STIR-FRY

This is a wonderful one-dish main course. Even though coconut milk is high in fat, it makes a silky smooth sauce and, for people who are lactose intolerant, it is a real treat!

The whole chiles are traditional in Thai cooking, but they are in the dish to add flavour only. If you are worried that your guests might eat them, you can use one chopped jalapeño instead—cook it with the onion and garlic.

SERVES 4 TO 6

2 tbsp	vegetable oil	25 mL
I lb	boneless, skinless chicken breasts, cut into 1½-inch/7 cm chunks	500 g
I	onion, thinly sliced	I
2	cloves garlic, finely chopped	2
I tbsp	chopped fresh ginger root	15 mL
I tsp	curry powder	5 mL
I tbsp	Thai fish sauce	15 mL
⅓ cup	chicken stock or water	75 mL
1½ cups	coconut milk	375 mL
12	small hot green chiles, whole	12
	Handful Thai basil or regular basil	
½ lb	rice vermicelli, soaked, or cooked wheat noodles (angelhair or linguine)	250 g
	Salt and freshly ground pepper to taste	

1. Heat the oil in a wok. Add the chicken and stir-fry just until the chicken loses its raw appearance.

2. Add the onion, garlic and ginger. Stir-fry for 30 to 60 seconds.

3. Stir in the curry powder, fish sauce, chicken stock and coconut milk. Bring to a boil.

4. Add the whole chiles and basil and cook for 3 to 4 minutes.

5. Add the noodles and combine well. Cook until the noodles are thoroughly heated. Taste for seasoning and add salt and pepper if necessary.

LOWER-FAT VERSION: *Use only 1 tbsp/15 mL oil to begin the stir-fry. Use 1½ cups/375 mL pureed tomatoes instead of the coconut milk, or use half tomatoes and half coconut milk. Thin the sauce with water if it is too thick.*

CHEESE TART WITH YEAST PASTRY

This is an interesting version of quiche made with an easy, rich yeast crust.

SERVES 8 TO 10

YEAST CRUST

2 cups	all-purpose flour	500 mL
I	package dry yeast	I
½ cup	warm milk	125 mL
2	eggs, beaten	2
I tsp	salt	5 mL
⅓ cup	unsalted butter, at room temperature	75 mL

FILLING

6 oz	diced ham	175 g
6 oz	Swiss cheese, grated	175 g
2	eggs	2
2	egg yolks	2
I cup	whipping cream or crème fraîche	250 mL
	Salt and freshly ground pepper to taste	
pinch	nutmeg	pinch
2 tbsp	unsalted butter, cut into bits	25 mL

1. Sift the flour into a bowl and make a well in the centre. Add the yeast. Pour half the milk over the yeast and allow it to dissolve, about 5 minutes.

2. Stir in the rest of the milk, 2 eggs and 1 tsp/5 mL salt. Gather the dough together with your fingers. (The dough will be very moist and sticky.) Knead the dough for about 5 minutes by slapping it against the sides of the bowl. Beat in ⅓ cup/75 mL butter. (The dough may still be sticky.)

3. Place the dough in an oiled bowl, cover and allow to rise in a warm place for 1 to 1½ hours, or until doubled in bulk.

4. When the dough has risen, punch it down and place in a 10-inch/25 cm spring-form pan. Flatten the dough with your hands and push it up the sides of the pan to line it. Do not worry if the dough doesn't stay perfectly where you press it.

5. Arrange the ham and cheese over the bottom of the dough. Beat 2 eggs with the egg yolks, cream, salt, pepper and nutmeg. Pour over the ham and cheese. Dot with 2 tbsp/25 mL butter. Allow to rest for 15 minutes before baking.

6. Preheat the oven to 400°F/200°C. Bake for 1 hour, or until the filling is brown and the pastry is crisp. Serve hot, warm or cold.

LOWER-FAT VERSION: *Use only 3 tbsp/45 mL butter in the dough. In the filling, omit the butter and use half the ham and cheese. Use 3 whole eggs instead of 2 eggs and 2 yolks. Use milk instead of whipping cream.*

CARAMELIZED APPLE PANCAKES

This makes two or three 8-inch/20 cm pancakes. Some people like to eat a whole one, but half is usually enough. Serve with maple syrup. (The batter, without the caramelized apples, makes wonderful pancakes on its own.)

SERVES 4 TO 6

2	medium apples	2
½ cup	granulated sugar	125 mL
2 tbsp	unsalted butter	25 mL
2	eggs	2
1½ cups	buttermilk	375 mL
1 cup	all-purpose flour	250 mL
¾ tsp	baking soda	4 mL
¼ tsp	salt	1 mL
2 tbsp	granulated sugar	25 mL
¼ cup	unsalted butter	50 mL

1. Peel the apples and cut them in half. Core and slice thinly.

2. Place ½ cup/125 mL sugar in a heavy skillet and heat until it begins to turn a caramel colour. Do not stir. Add 2 tbsp/25 mL butter. Stir until melted. Do not worry if the mixture is lumpy.

3. Add the apples and cook them until tender, about 10 minutes. Stir occasionally. Reserve. Juices should have evaporated and apples should be in a thick syrup.

4. Prepare the pancake batter by beating the eggs with the buttermilk. Sift or mix together the flour, baking soda, salt and 2 tbsp/25 mL sugar. Stir into the egg mixture.

5. Melt ¼ cup/50 mL butter in an 8-inch/20 cm or 9-inch/23 cm omelette pan, crêpe pan or non-stick pan. Stir the melted butter into the batter.

6. Place about ½ cup/125 mL batter in the hot pan. Cook a little and then arrange some of the apples on top. Pour more batter on to cover the apples—about another ½ cup/125 mL. Cook for a few minutes.

7. Slip the pancake out of the pan onto a plate and then flip it back into pan to cook the other side. Cook for another few minutes.

8. Repeat with the remaining batter and apples. If you have extra apples, serve them over the pancakes.

   LOWER-FAT VERSION: *Use 1 tbsp/15 mL butter to cook the apples. Use only 2 tbsp/25 mL butter in the batter.*

Yogurt Pancakes

This is a great recipe to make with your kids, and if you use a plastic ketchup or mustard container to pipe the batter into fancy shapes, they'll love them even more. (You can use buttermilk in place of yogurt but the batter will be thinner.)

MAKES APPROX. 20

2	eggs	2
1½ cups	unflavoured yogurt	375 mL
2 tbsp	granulated sugar (optional)	25 mL
¼ tsp	salt (optional)	1 mL
1 cup	all-purpose flour	250 mL
1 tsp	baking soda	5 mL
2 tbsp	unsalted butter	25 mL
	Chocolate chips (optional)	
	Raisins (optional)	
	Fresh blueberries (optional)	

1. Break the eggs into a bowl and add the yogurt. Stir with a whisk. Stir in the sugar and salt if you are using them.

2. Sift the flour and baking soda into the egg mixture. Stir just until ingredients are mixed.

3. Melt the butter in a large skillet and pour it into the batter carefully. Mix in.

4. Return the pan to the heat. The pancakes can be made into rounds by dropping spoonfuls of batter into the pan. Happy faces or designs can be made with chocolate chips, raisins or blueberries. Numbers, letters, fish or boats can be made by pouring batter into a plastic ketchup bottle and writing with the batter directly in the pan.

5. Cook the pancakes for about 2 minutes, or until tiny bubbles appear and the surface has lost its sheen. Flip and cook the second side briefly. (Turn the letters and numbers over again before serving so they will be going in the right direction!) Serve with maple syrup, jam or corn syrup.

SMOKED CHEESE AND CHILI FRITTATA

Smoked cheese adds a fabulous taste to pizza, quesadillas, tacos, pasta and casseroles. This frittata can be served hot or cold, in little squares as an appetizer or in larger pieces as a main course with a salad and cornbread (see page 124). It can also be served in pita or foccacia as a sandwich, or as small "croutons" in a salad.

SERVES 8

1 tbsp	unsalted butter, at room temperature	15 mL
¼ cup	dry breadcrumbs	50 mL
½ cup	all-purpose flour	125 mL
1 tsp	baking powder	5 mL
10	eggs	10
2 cups	cottage cheese	500 mL
3 cups	grated smoked mozzarella or Monterey Jack cheese	750 mL
¼ cup	unsalted butter, melted	50 mL
½ cup	diced mild green chiles	125 mL
1	jalapeño chile, finely chopped (optional)	1
1 tsp	salt	5 mL
½ tsp	freshly ground pepper	2 mL
½ cup	chopped fresh cilantro	125 mL
¼ cup	chopped fresh chives	50 mL

1. Preheat the oven to 350°F/180°C. Brush a 13- x 9-inch/3 L baking dish with the butter and sprinkle with breadcrumbs.

2. Combine the flour and baking powder.

3. Beat the eggs together in a large bowl. Whisk in the flour mixture, cottage cheese, grated cheese, melted butter, mild chiles, jalapeño, salt, pepper, cilantro and chives.

4. Pour the mixture into the baking dish and bake for 40 to 45 minutes, or until set. Let cool for 10 minutes before serving.

LOWER-FAT VERSION: *Omit all the butter in the recipe. Lightly oil the baking dish and sprinkle with breadcrumbs. Use 5 whole eggs and 10 egg whites instead of 10 whole eggs. Use low-fat pressed cottage cheese and only half the smoked cheese.*

WILD MUSHROOM AND FONTINA PIZZA

This pizza can be served as an appetizer or as a main course with a salad. If you cannot find wild mushrooms (such as portobello, shitake, oyster, morels, chanterelles or a combination), simply use regular ones.

SERVES 4 TO 6

I	10-inch/25 cm foccacia, approximately	I
¼ cup	olive oil	50 mL
4	cloves garlic, finely chopped	4
I lb	fresh wild mushrooms, sliced	500 g
I tsp	chopped fresh rosemary (or pinch dried)	5 mL
I tsp	salt	5 mL
½ tsp	freshly ground pepper	2 mL
2 cups	grated Fontina cheese	500 mL
¼ cup	chopped fresh basil	50 mL

1. Preheat the oven to 400°F/200°C. Cut the foccacia in half horizontally. Brush the cut surface with half the olive oil. Bake the bread cut side up on a baking sheet for 8 to 10 for 10 minutes, or until lightly toasted.

2. Meanwhile, heat the remaining olive oil in a large skillet. Add the garlic, mushrooms, rosemary, salt and pepper. Cook for 5 to 10 minutes, or until wilted.

3. Spread the mushroom mixture over the cut side of the bread. Sprinkle with cheese and basil. Bake for 6 to 10 minutes, or just until the cheese melts and bubbles. Cut into wedges to serve.

RISOTTO WITH PANCETTA AND RAPINI

Risotto is a very special Italian rice dish that tastes rich and creamy (although it does not usually contain cream). The texture is achieved by using short-grain Italian rice that absorbs a large amount of liquid and by adding the liquid slowly as the rice cooks stirring constantly so that the grains of rice rub together.

Risotto must be made just before serving, so I like to serve it as the first sit-down dish (I make it for guests who I do not mind being in the kitchen with me as I cook).

Leftover risotto is delicious cooked like a pancake. Add an egg or two and cook in butter or olive oil until crisp on both sides. Cut the pancake in wedges and serve it with a salad.

SERVES 6 TO 8

I lb	rapini, trimmed and chopped	500 g
¼ cup	olive oil	50 mL
2	cloves garlic, finely chopped	2
I	onion, chopped	I
2 oz	pancetta, diced	60 g
pinch	hot red chili flakes	pinch
2 cups	short-grain rice (preferably Arborio)	500 mL
6 cups	chicken stock, hot (approx.)	1.5 L
I tsp	salt	5 mL
½ tsp	freshly ground pepper	2 mL
2 tbsp	unsalted butter	25 mL
½ cup	grated Parmesan cheese (preferably Parmigiano Reggiano)	125 mL

1. Cook the rapini in a pot of boiling salted water for 5 minutes. Rinse with cold water and drain well. Reserve.

2. Heat the oil in a large, deep skillet. Add the garlic, onion, pancetta and hot chili flakes. Cook until the onion and garlic are tender and the pancetta is cooked.

3. Add the rapini and combine well. Cook for 2 minutes.

4. Add the rice. Stir to coat the rice well with the oil and vegetables (the dish can be made ahead up to this point).

5. Add a ladleful of chicken stock. Cook over medium or medium-high heat until the stock evaporates or is absorbed before you add the next ladleful of stock. Stir almost constantly. Continue to cook and add stock until the rice is barely tender. This should take about 15 minutes. You may or may not have to use all the stock. Add the salt and pepper.

6. Stir in the butter and cheese. Taste and adjust the seasonings if necessary. Serve immediately.

LOWER-FAT VERSION: *Use only half the olive oil. Use half the pancetta, or omit it entirely. Omit the butter. Use half the cheese.*

VEGETABLES

Swiss Chard Italian Style

Swiss chard is an unusual vegetable, because you can use both the tender green leaves and the tougher stalks. I like to cook the two parts separately because of their very different nature. These two dishes can be served at the same meal or separately. Instead of the Swiss chard stalks, fennel, celery or leeks could be used. Instead of the Swiss chard greens, spinach could be used.

SERVES 6

2 lb	Swiss chard	1 kg
	Salt and freshly ground pepper to taste	
¼ cup	unsalted butter	50 mL
¼ cup	grated Parmesan cheese (preferably Parmigiano Reggiano)	50 mL
2	cloves garlic, finely chopped	2

1. Preheat the oven to 350°F/180°C.

2. Cut the leaves of Swiss chard from the stalks (see illustration). Break the leaves up into pieces and wash and dry them well. Reserve.

3. Cut the stalks into 2-inch/5 cm pieces. Wash them well. Cook in boiling water for 10 minutes, or until tender. Drain well.

4. Place the stalks in a buttered gratin dish and sprinkle with salt and pepper. Dot with half the butter and all the cheese. Bake for 30 minutes and serve.

5. To prepare the leaves, melt the remaining butter in a large skillet. Cook the garlic until tender and fragrant but do not brown. Add the leaves and cook for about 6 minutes, until wilted and tender. Sprinkle with salt and pepper and serve.

LOWER-FAT VERSION: *Use 1 tbsp/15 mL olive oil to cook the garlic and Swiss chard leaves. Use half the butter and cheese when baking the stalks.*

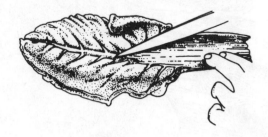

ASPARAGUS MARCO POLO

This recipe is adapted from one presented by James Barber, Vancouver based cookbook author and television celebrity, at the 1986 March of Dimes Celebrity Gourmet Gala. It is one of the best ways I have ever had asparagus. It can be served hot or cold.

When James Barber explained how to cut the asparagus for this recipe, he said to place the asparagus in line with 12 o'clock and 6 o'clock and to cut it at an 11 o'clock angle. I found it easier to place the asparagus in line with 9 o'clock and 3 o'clock and to cut at a 10 o'clock angle (if you're left-handed it's probably completely different!). When I originally described this recipe on the radio, these instructions sounded especially crazy (and they don't sound much better here!), but in the end it doesn't really matter.

SERVES 4 TO 6

1½ lb	asparagus	750 g
3 tbsp	vegetable oil	45 mL
2 tbsp	fresh ginger root, cut into tiny matchstick pieces	25 mL
½ tsp	salt	2 mL
1 tsp	granulated sugar	5 mL
2 tbsp	lemon juice	25 mL

1. Cut off the tough stems of the asparagus. If you wish, peel the stems partway up with a vegetable peeler.

2. Cut the asparagus into pieces about ½ inch/1 cm thick, on a sharp diagonal or as described above (see also illustration).

3. Heat the oil in a skillet. Add the ginger and cook for a few seconds until fragrant.

4. Add the asparagus, sprinkle with the salt and toss with the oil. Cook for 1 to 2 minutes. Add the sugar, toss, cover and cook for 2 to 3 minutes.

5. Add the lemon juice. Toss well and serve.

SPINACH WITH RAISINS AND PINE NUTS

This unusual combination of flavours with spinach is quite common in Spain and Italy, but not often found here. Even if you do not like anchovies, they taste great used as a seasoning in this recipe. Freeze the rest of the package for another use.

SERVES 4

1½ lb	spinach	750 g
½ cup	raisins	125 mL
1 cup	boiling water	250 mL
⅓ cup	pine nuts, lightly toasted	75 mL
2 tbsp	olive oil	25 mL
2	cloves garlic, finely chopped	2
4	anchovy fillets, finely chopped	4
	Salt and freshly ground pepper to taste	

1. Preheat the oven to 350°F/180°C.

2. Remove and discard the tough stems from the spinach. Wash the spinach well and place it in a large pot with just the water from the washing clinging to the leaves. Cover and cook just until wilted. Cool and gently squeeze out the excess water with your hands. Chop coarsely.

3. Meanwhile, place the raisins in a bowl, cover with the boiling water and soak for 10 minutes. Drain.

4. Just before serving, heat the oil in a skillet and add the garlic and anchovies. Cook on medium heat until fragrant, but do not brown. Add the raisins and spinach and toss well until the spinach is thoroughly heated. Season with salt and pepper if necessary (anchovies are very salty). Sprinkle with the toasted pine nuts.

LOWER-FAT VERSION: *Use 2 tsp/10 mL olive oil to cook the garlic and anchovies. Use only 2 tbsp/25 mL pine nuts.*

MIXED RED, YELLOW AND GREEN PEPPERS

You can serve this as an appetizer or salad with a little red wine vinegar, garlic, capers, chopped anchovies and olive oil. (If you are serving it as a salad or appetizer, simply char and peel the peppers and combine with the above ingredients. They do not need further cooking.) You can also serve this as a topping for pasta or on veal or chicken. As a vegetable, it goes beautifully with any plainly cooked roast or chop.

If you cannot find red, yellow and green peppers, just use more of the colours you can find.

SERVES 6 TO 8

4	red peppers	4
4	green peppers	4
4	yellow peppers	4
2 tbsp	olive oil	25 mL
3	cloves garlic, finely chopped	3
¼ tsp	hot red chili flakes	1 mL
½ tsp	salt	2 mL
½ tsp	freshly ground pepper	2 mL
¼ cup	chopped fresh basil or parsley	50 mL

1. Cut the peppers in half and remove the ribs and seeds. Place cut side down on a baking sheet and broil until they are black and charred. (If you are barbecuing the peppers, leave them whole, place them on the barbecue and turn until they are charred all over. Remove the ribs and seeds when the peppers have cooled.)

2. Cool the peppers and peel off the blackened skin. (Some people put the peppers in a paper or plastic bag to cool—they feel the skins come off more easily—but I find it makes little difference.)

3. Cut the peppers into large pieces.

4. Heat the oil in large skillet and add the garlic and hot chili flakes. Add the peppers and cook for 10 to 15 minutes. Season with salt, pepper and basil.

LOWER-FAT VERSION: *Use only 1 tbsp/15 mL oil or less to cook the garlic and peppers.*

CHEESE-BAKED VEGETABLE CUSTARD

*This recipe is roughly based on one taught at Lydie Marshall's wonderful
cooking school in New York City. Her large, warm, French-Provincial kitchen
in the basement of her brownstone welcomes students with its friendly
aromas. This delicious custard is full of vegetables and cheese.*

SERVES 6 TO 8

2 tbsp	unsalted butter	25 mL
8 oz	bacon, diced	250 g
2	onions, chopped	2
2	cloves garlic, finely chopped	2
2	leeks, trimmed and sliced	2
1 lb	cabbage, chopped, cooked and drained	500 g
2 lb	spinach, washed, cooked, squeezed dry and coarsely chopped	1 kg
4	eggs	4
1 cup	whipping cream, light cream or milk	250 mL
1½ tsp	salt	7 mL
¼ tsp	freshly ground pepper	1 mL
1 cup	grated Swiss cheese (approx. 4 oz/125 g)	250 mL
¼ cup	grated Parmesan cheese (preferably Parmigiano Reggiano)	50 mL

1. Preheat the oven to 375°F/190°C.

2. Heat the butter in a skillet and cook the bacon until crisp. Remove the bacon and discard all but ¼ cup/50 mL of fat from pan.

3. Cook the onions, garlic and leeks in the bacon fat until tender. Stir in the cabbage and spinach.

4. In a large bowl, beat the eggs with the cream, salt and pepper. Add the vegetables, reserved bacon bits and Swiss cheese.

5. Transfer the mixture to a buttered 3-qt/3 L shallow casserole dish and sprinkle with Parmesan. Bake for 1 hour.

LOWER-FAT VERSION: *Omit the butter and bacon. Use 2 tbsp/25 mL olive oil to cook the onions. Use low-fat milk instead of cream in the custard.*

CURRIED PUREED PARSNIPS

When this recipe was aired on the radio, I told everyone that I felt sorry for parsnips, and that even though this was one of the most delicious vegetable dishes I had ever tasted, I didn't think anyone would write in for the recipe. To our surprise and delight, lots of people asked for the recipe, saying that they liked parsnips or were looking for a recipe to try them. We even received thank-you notes from people who tried this and loved it!

This recipe can also be made with carrots, turnips or sweet potatoes, or a combination of pureed vegetables.

SERVES 6 TO 8

2 lb	parsnips, cleaned and sliced	1 kg
2 tbsp	unsalted butter	25 mL
2	cloves garlic, finely chopped	2
2 tsp	curry powder	10 mL
½ tsp	cinnamon	2 mL
pinch	nutmeg	pinch
1 tsp	salt	5 mL
¼ tsp	freshly ground pepper	1 mL
½ cup	whipping cream, light cream, or milk	125 mL

1. Steam or boil the parsnips until they are tender, about 15 minutes. Drain them well.

2. Melt the butter in a small saucepan and add the garlic. Cook for a few minutes over medium-low heat until very fragrant and tender. Do not brown. Add the curry powder, cinnamon and nutmeg. Cook for a few minutes to release the flavours. Do not allow the mixture to burn.

3. Add the salt, pepper and cream to the mixture and heat well.

4. Puree or mash the cooked parsnips with the cream mixture until smooth. Taste and adjust the seasonings if necessary. Serve immediately or pipe or spread in a baking dish, cover with buttered parchment paper and reheat at 375°F/190°C for 20 to 25 minutes.

LOWER-FAT VERSION: *Use 1 tbsp/15 mL olive oil to cook the garlic. Use low-fat milk.*

CANDIED SWEET POTATOES

This Southern-style sweet-potato dish is great with any plain roast or meat. The potatoes can be served mashed or plain (if I overcook the potatoes by accident, I mash them!).

SERVES 6

2 lb	sweet potatoes	1 kg
¼ cup	unsalted butter	50 mL
¼ cup	brown sugar	50 mL
¼ cup	orange juice	50 mL
½ tsp	salt	2 mL
½ tsp	cinnamon	2 mL
½ tsp	ginger	2 mL
pinch	allspice	pinch
pinch	nutmeg	pinch

1. Peel the sweet potatoes and cut them in half. Cover with water, bring to a boil and cook for 10 to 15 minutes, or until about two-thirds cooked.

2. In a wide saucepan, melt the butter and add the remaining ingredients.

3. Cut the sweet potatoes into 2-inch/5 cm cubes and add to the butter mixture. Combine well.

4. Cook over medium heat for 10 to 15 minutes, or until the liquid evaporates and the potatoes are cooked thoroughly and glazed. Serve as is or mash and spread in a casserole dish.

LOWER-FAT VERSION: *Use half the butter, or omit it entirely.*

Bulgur Wheat Pilaf

If you are tired of the vegetable dishes you have been serving lately, try this delicious alternative to rice. Bulgur is a staple in the Middle East and is actually cracked wheat that has been steamed and dried. If you have trouble finding it in the cereal section of a supermarket, try bulk food stores, health food stores or Middle Eastern specialty shops. It comes in three sizes—for this recipe you'll need medium or large grains.

SERVES 4 TO 6

1 tbsp	olive oil	15 mL
1	large red onion, diced	1
1	clove garlic, finely chopped	1
1½ cups	medium- or large-grain bulgur wheat	375 mL
2½ cups	chicken stock, hot	625 mL
	Salt and freshly ground pepper to taste	
3 tbsp	chopped fresh parsley	45 mL
3 tbsp	chopped fresh dill	45 mL

1. Heat the oil in a large saucepan or wide, deep skillet. Add the onion and garlic and cook until tender and fragrant but do not brown.

2. Add the bulgur and combine with the onion mixture, coating the grains well with the oil.

3. Add the stock, bring to a boil and then reduce the heat to low. Cover and simmer gently for 15 to 20 minutes, or until all the liquid is absorbed.

4. Add some salt and pepper, the parsley and dill. Stir together gently. Taste and adjust seasonings if necessary.

BARBECUED POTATOES AND ONIONS

This is the perfect addition to any barbecue. I usually barbecue the potatoes before cooking the meat or fish and then keep them warm on the barbecue or in the oven while I'm preparing the rest of the meal. You can also use regular potatoes and regular cooking onions. The onions almost burn (sometimes they do!) and caramelize. The potatoes are tender and sweet from the onions.

You can add different things to this—basil, dill, parsley, cream, sour cream or yogurt. Just make up your own version. Peter Gzowski, the host of Morningside (where I'm an occasional guest), says this is one of his favourite recipes.

SERVES 3 TO 4

2 lb	baking potatoes	1 kg
2	red onions, sliced	2
	Salt and freshly ground pepper to taste	
½ tsp	dried rosemary or 1 tsp/5 mL fresh rosemary	2 mL
¼ cup	unsalted butter, cut into bits	50 mL

1. Peel the potatoes and slice them ½ inch/1 cm thick.

2. Butter the middle of a 24-inch/60 cm piece of heavy-duty aluminum foil.

3. Arrange a layer of potatoes on the buttered section of foil. Top with a layer of onions. Season with salt, pepper and ¼ tsp/1 mL rosemary and dot with half the butter. Top with the remaining potatoes, onions, seasonings and butter. (Don't have more than two layers of potatoes, or they won't brown.)

4. Close the package tightly. Barbecue or grill for about 20 minutes. Turn the package and cook for 20 minutes longer.

   LOWER-FAT VERSION: *Use 2 tbsp/25 mL olive oil instead of the butter.*

MASHED POTATOES WITH WILD MUSHROOMS

Mashed potatoes are making a big comeback, but with style. Flavour plain mashed potatoes with a few spoonfuls of pesto sauce (see page 85) or olivada (see page 21), or make these wonderful mashed potatoes with wild mushrooms.

SERVES 4 TO 6

2 lb	baking potatoes	I kg
I oz	dried wild mushrooms	30 g
I cup	boiling water	250 mL
2 tbsp	unsalted butter	25 mL
I	onion, diced	I
I	clove garlic, finely chopped	I
8 oz	fresh mushrooms, sliced	250 g
¾ cup	whipping cream	175 mL
	Salt and freshly ground pepper to taste	
½ cup	grated Parmesan cheese (preferably Parmigiano Reggiano)	125 mL

1. Peel the potatoes and cut them into 2-inch/5 cm pieces. Cover with cold water, bring to a boil and simmer until tender, about 20 minutes.

2. Meanwhile, place the dried wild mushrooms in a bowl and cover with the boiling water. Allow to soak for 20 minutes. Strain the soaking liquid through a paper towel-lined sieve to remove any sand or grit. Reserve the liquid. Rinse the mushrooms and chop. Reserve.

3. Melt the butter in a large skillet and add the onion and garlic. Cook until browned.

4. Add the fresh and wild mushrooms and cook until any liquid released from mushrooms evaporates. Add the soaking liquid from the mushrooms and cook until the liquid is absorbed.

5. Add the cream and bring to a boil.

6. When the potatoes are tender, drain and pat dry. Mash potatoes with masher, food mill or potato ricer. Beat in the mushroom mixture. Season to taste with salt and pepper and add the cheese. Serve immediately or spoon into a buttered casserole dish. Brush the top with a little melted butter and reheat at 350°F/180°C for 20 minutes just before serving.

LOWER-FAT VERSION: *Use 1 tbsp/15 mL olive oil instead of the butter. Use milk instead of whipping cream. Use half the amount of cheese.*

POTATO LATKES (POTATO PANCAKES)

Potato latkes or pancakes are one of the most delicious of all Jewish festival foods. They're so delicious, in fact, that they are finally in vogue. I've seen many restaurants serve mini potato pancakes, topped with sour cream and caviar, as an appetizer.

Potato pancakes should be served as soon as they are cooked, with sour cream or applesauce. They can be served as an appetizer, main course or side dish.

MAKES 16 3-INCH/7.5 CM PANCAKES

2	eggs	2
I	small onion, finely chopped or grated	I
3	large baking potatoes, peeled	3
I tsp	salt	5 mL
¼ tsp	freshly ground pepper	I mL
3 tbsp	matzo meal or cornflake crumbs	50 mL
	Oil for frying	

1. Combine the eggs with the onion.

2. Grate the potatoes into the egg mixture and stir well to prevent discolouration. (If you are doing this in a food processor, simply chop the onion with the steel knife, blend in the eggs and add the potatoes in chunks. Process until the potatoes are finely chopped.)

3. Add the salt, pepper and matzo meal.

4. Heat enough oil in a large skillet to measure ½ inch/1 cm deep. Add the batter to the oil by the spoonful and flatten each pancake with the back of the spoon. Cook until crisp, then turn and cook the second side.

5. Drain the pancakes on paper towels as they are ready. (When you cook each batch, add more oil if necessary, but add the oil between batches, and not while the pancakes are cooking.)

Rice Pilaf

This is a basic rice pilaf, but many other vegetables can be added to it. In a pilaf, the rice is usually coated in butter or oil (usually with onions and/or other vegetables) and then cooked in twice the amount of liquid. Unless you are using converted rice, rinse the rice in a sieve until the water runs clear. To cook brown rice, use an extra ½ cup/125 mL liquid and cook for 45 to 50 minutes.

To shape the cooked pilaf in a ring, butter a ring mould generously and spoon the rice in firmly. Cover with buttered parchment paper and keep warm in a very low oven until serving time. Invert onto a serving plate.

SERVES 4 TO 6

2 tbsp	unsalted butter or olive oil	25 mL
I	onion, finely chopped	I
I	clove garlic, finely chopped	I
I	red pepper, diced	I
¼ lb	mushrooms, sliced	125 g
I cup	long-grain white rice, rinsed	250 mL
2 cups	chicken stock, hot	500 mL
	Salt and freshly ground pepper to taste	
2 tbsp	unsalted butter (optional)	25 mL
2 tbsp	chopped fresh parsley or other fresh herbs	25 mL

1. Heat 2 tbsp/25 mL butter in a large saucepan. Add the onion and garlic and cook until tender, about 5 minutes.

2. Add the red pepper and mushrooms and combine well. Cook for another 5 minutes.

3. Add the rice and coat well with the vegetables. Stir in the stock and bring to a boil. Season lightly with salt and pepper. Cover, lower the heat and cook for 20 to 25 minutes, or until the rice is tender and the liquid is absorbed.

4. Stir in 2 tbsp/25 mL butter and the parsley. Adjust the seasonings to taste.

LOWER-FAT VERSION: *Start the vegetables in 1 tbsp/15 mL olive oil. Omit the butter at the end.*

QUICK RED BEANS AND RICE

Versions of this dish are very common in the Caribbean. Although it is usually made with dried beans, using canned or precooked ones shortens the cooking time dramatically!

This can be served as a main course or side dish.

SERVES 4 TO 6

I tbsp	vegetable oil	15 mL
2	slices bacon, diced	2
I	onion, chopped	I
I	clove garlic, finely chopped	I
I	jalapeño chile, chopped	I
I	14-oz/398 mL tin red kidney beans, drained (or approx. 1 ½ cups/375 mL cooked red beans)	I
1 ½ cups	fragrant or long-grain rice, rinsed	375 mL
2 cups	water	500 mL
I cup	coconut milk	250 mL
I tsp	salt	5 mL

1. Place the oil and bacon in a large saucepan and cook until the fat renders out of the bacon. Discard all but 2 tbsp/25 mL fat.

2. Add the onion, garlic and jalapeño. Cook for a few minutes until tender and fragrant.

3. Add the beans and the rice. Combine well. Add the water and coconut milk. Bring to a boil. Cover and cook gently for 20 minutes. Fluff gently.

LOWER-FAT VERSION: *Omit the bacon. Replace half the coconut milk with additional water.*

SALADS AND SALAD DRESSINGS

Marinated Vegetable Salad with Balsamic Vinegar Dressing

Balsamic vinegar is a sweet-tasting vinegar made by aging the juice of Trebbiano grapes in different kinds of wood—oak, chestnut, mulberry and juniper among others. When I visited the Fini factory outside Milan, we were taken into the vinegar "caves" and allowed to taste balsamic vinegar that was 150 years old. You can sometimes buy these aged vinegars in specialty food shops for exorbitant prices, and balsamic vinegar tastings have become as elitist as some wine tastings. However, even the "ordinary" balsamic vinegar can be quite delicious—as long as you're not tasting it next to the 150-year-old variety!

Not only is this salad delicious, but it is really beautiful to look at. After the vegetables are cooked, plunge them into cold water to set the colour and texture. If you prefer a less-organized salad, simply toss all the vegetables with the dressing. It looks gorgeous this way, too.

SERVES 8 TO 10

I	small head cauliflower	I
I	small bunch broccoli	I
I lb	asparagus or green beans	500 g
I lb	carrots	500 g
2	tomatoes	2
I	bulb fresh fennel, trimmed and sliced	I
½ cup	black olives	125 mL
¼ cup	chopped fresh basil or parsley	50 mL

BALSAMIC VINEGAR DRESSING

¼ cup	balsamic vinegar	50 mL
½ tsp	salt	2 mL
¼ tsp	freshly ground pepper	I mL
I	clove garlic, minced	I
I tsp	Dijon mustard	5 mL
4	anchovy fillets, minced (optional)	4
½ cup	olive oil (or more)	125 mL

1. Separate the cauliflower and broccoli into florets. Trim the tough bases off the asparagus and peel 1 inch/2.5 cm up the stems. (If you are using beans, simply trim them.) Peel the carrots if necessary and cut into 2-inch/5 cm sticks.

2. Cook each vegetable separately, until tender-crisp. Chill in ice water and pat dry.

3. Arrange the vegetables in sections on a large dish. Slice the tomatoes into wedges and arrange beside the other vegetables with the fennel. Sprinkle with the olives and chopped basil.

4. Prepare the dressing by whisking the vinegar with the salt, pepper, garlic, mustard and anchovies. Whisk in the oil. Taste and adjust the seasonings if necessary. Drizzle the dressing evenly over the vegetables and allow to marinate until ready to serve. (The salad can be eaten immediately, but will have a more intense taste if it is allowed to marinate for 1 to 2 hours.)

Tomatoes with Basil Parmesan Dressing

The most delicious Parmesan cheese is Parmigiano Reggiano. It is never hard, bitter, salty or soapy like some Parmesan.

Ripe tomatoes and fresh basil are the perfect way to welcome summer. If you cannot find fresh basil, use fresh parsley; do not substitute dry.

SERVES 6

8	large ripe tomatoes	8
¼ cup	grated or thinly sliced Parmesan cheese (preferably Parmigiano Reggiano)	50 mL
¼ cup	chopped fresh basil	50 mL
	Salt and freshly ground pepper to taste	
¼ cup	red wine vinegar or balsamic vinegar	50 mL
¼ cup	olive oil	50 mL

1. Cut the tomatoes into slices ½ inch/1 cm thick. Sprinkle with the cheese and basil.

2. Combine the salt, pepper, vinegar and oil and pour over the tomatoes.

3. Refrigerate for 1 hour, or until serving time. Toss.

POTATO SALAD WITH OLIVES AND CHOPPED CHIVES

Good potato salad is always a favourite. Serve this warm or at room temperature, as the olive oil will solidify slightly when refrigerated.

SERVES 6 TO 8

DRESSING

¼ cup	white wine vinegar	50 mL
I	clove garlic, minced	I
2 tbsp	Dijon mustard	25 mL
½ tsp	salt	2 mL
¼ tsp	freshly ground pepper	I mL
½ cup	olive oil	125 mL

SALAD

3 lb	red-skinned potatoes or new potatoes	1.5 kg
¼ cup	white wine vinegar	50 mL
½ tsp	salt	2 mL
½ cup	black olives	125 mL
¼ cup	chopped fresh chives or green onions	50 mL
3	hard-cooked eggs, cut into chunks	3

1. To prepare the dressing, combine ¼ cup/50 mL vinegar, garlic, mustard, salt and pepper in a bowl and whisk together. Whisk in the oil and taste the dressing. Adjust the seasonings if necessary.

2. Peel the potatoes. Cut them in half if they are large.

3. Place the potatoes in cold water with ¼ cup/50 mL vinegar and ½ tsp/2 mL salt. Bring to a boil. Simmer until tender, about 20 to 30 minutes.

4. As soon as the potatoes are cooked, drain well and toss with the dressing.

5. Add the olives, chives and eggs and allow to marinate until ready to serve, tossing occasionally. Serve warm or at room temperature.

   LOWER-FAT VERSION: *Use ¼ cup/50 mL oil. Use half or omit the olives. Use only hard-cooked egg whites.*

Designer Salad
with Raspberry Dressing

"Designer" lettuces are very in vogue now. If they are hard to find, use this delicious dressing on Romaine or your favourite salad greens.

SERVES 6 TO 8

I	small head Boston lettuce	I
I	small head radicchio or ruby lettuce	I
2	heads Belgian endive	2
I	bunch arugula (sometimes called rocket)	I

DRESSING

3 tbsp	red or white wine vinegar or raspberry vinegar	45 mL
3 tbsp	whipping cream	45 mL
½ tsp	salt	2 mL
¼ tsp	freshly ground pepper	I mL
⅓ cup	olive oil (or more)	75 mL

1. Wash the lettuces well and break into bite-sized pieces. Dry them thoroughly and place in a salad bowl.

2. To make the dressing, place the vinegar in a bowl and whisk in the cream, salt and pepper. Whisk until frothy. Slowly beat in the oil. Taste and adjust the seasonings (the dressing should be creamy).

3. Just before serving, toss the lettuce with the dressing.

SALAD NIÇOISE

This is a slightly off-beat version of Salad Niçoise. Instead of being in the salad, the tuna is pureed into a creamy dressing that is also delicious on cold chicken, veal or turkey.

SERVES 6 TO 8

DRESSING

1	small tin anchovy fillets (about 8)	1
1	6½-oz/184 g tin tuna	1
½ cup	mayonnaise	125 mL
½ cup	sour cream	125 mL

SALAD

1	head Romaine lettuce	1
5	potatoes, cooked and sliced	5
1 lb	green beans, cooked	500 g
4	tomatoes, cut into wedges	4
3	hard-cooked eggs, chopped	3
½ cup	black olives	125 mL
1 tbsp	capers	15 mL
2 tbsp	chopped fresh parsley	25 mL
2 tbsp	finely chopped fresh tarragon (or ½ tsp/2 mL dried)	25 mL
3	green onions, chopped	3

1. Combine all the dressing ingredients in a blender or food processor. Taste and adjust seasonings if necessary.

2. Line a large salad bowl with the fullest lettuce leaves. Break up the remaining leaves and place in the bottom of the bowl.

3. Place the potato slices in the bowl and surround with the beans. Arrange the tomatoes and hard-cooked eggs around the outside edge of the salad.

4. Pour the dressing over the salad and sprinkle with the black olives, capers, parsley, tarragon and green onions.

   LOWER-FAT VERSION: *Use light mayonnaise and light sour cream or yogurt, and half the olives. Use only the whites of the hard-cooked eggs.*

Leftover Steak Salad with Mustard Dressing

I used to make this salad only with leftover steak, but we love it so much that now I cook steak especially for it.

You can leave the peppers as they are, peel them with a vegetable peeler or roast them (see page 99)—the peppers will be sweeter if they are roasted and peeled.

SERVES 6

1 lb	cooked steak or roast beef (preferably rare)	500 g
3	medium potatoes, cooked	3
1	red pepper	1
1	yellow pepper	1
6	green onions	6
4 oz	snow peas (optional)	125 g
	Any leftover cooked vegetables, such as asparagus, broccoli, beans, etc.	

MUSTARD DRESSING

3 tbsp	red wine vinegar, or sherry or balsamic vinegar	45 mL
1 tbsp	Dijon mustard	15 mL
½ cup	olive oil (or more)	125 mL
2 tbsp	finely chopped fresh tarragon (or ½ tsp/2 mL dried)	25 mL
	Salt and freshly ground pepper to taste	

1. Slice the steak or roast beef thinly.

2. Slice the potatoes and add to the steak. Cut the red and yellow peppers into julienne pieces and add to the steak.

3. Chop the green onions. Toss gently with the steak and potato mixture.

4. If you are using snow peas, blanch them for 1 minute, chill in cold water and pat dry. Reserve for a garnish or combine with the salad. Add any cooked vegetables.

5. Combine the ingredients for the dressing. Season to taste. Mix gently into the salad and eat immediately or allow to marinate in the refrigerator for a few hours. This salad tastes best served almost at room temperature, so remove it from the refrigerator about 30 minutes before serving.

LOWER-FAT VERSION: *Use flank steak (see p. 50) because it is a lean cut. Use sherry or balsamic vinegar and use half the oil.*

SMOKED CHICKEN SALAD

Smoked chicken is usually easy to find, but smoked turkey or ham could be used instead. This recipe could also be made with smoked salmon—use Honeycup or a Russian-style mustard instead of Dijon, and dill instead of basil.

SERVES 4 TO 6

1 lb	potatoes (approx. 3 medium)	500 g
1 lb	green beans or asparagus, cleaned and trimmed	500 g
3	tomatoes	3
1	head Romaine lettuce	1
1½ lb	smoked chicken (approx. ½ of a smoked chicken)	750 g

DRESSING

1 tbsp	Dijon mustard	15 mL
3 tbsp	red wine vinegar	45 mL
1 tsp	salt	5 mL
¼ tsp	freshly ground pepper	1 mL
½ cup	olive oil	125 mL
2 tbsp	chopped fresh basil or fresh parsley	25 mL

1. Boil the potatoes for 30 to 35 minutes, or until tender. Cool and slice.

2. Meanwhile, bring a deep skillet of water to the boil and add the beans or asparagus. Cook for 5 minutes. Drain and cool under cold water. Pat dry.

3. Slice the tomatoes and wash and dry the lettuce.

4. Remove the skin from the smoked chicken and separate the meat from the bones. Cut the meat into 1-inch/2.5 cm pieces. You will have approximately 1½ cups/ 375 mL of smoked chicken.

5. To assemble the salad, arrange the lettuce leaves over the bottom and up the sides of a large, flat salad bowl. Arrange the potatoes in the centre, the beans or asparagus around the potatoes, and the tomatoes around the outside edge. Place the chicken over the potatoes.

6. Prepare the dressing by whisking the mustard and vinegar together. Beat in the salt and pepper and then add the oil bit by bit. Add the basil. The dressing should be quite thick. Whisk again just before serving. Pour over the salad. Toss just before serving.

COLD SPAGHETTI SALAD

This is one of my favourite pasta salads. It makes a terrific light summer meal. (For more information on charring peppers, see page 99.)

SERVES 8

4	red peppers	4
4	yellow peppers	4
4	tomatoes, chopped	4
2	cloves garlic, minced	2
¼ tsp	hot red chili flakes	1 mL
½ cup	black olives	125 mL
2 tbsp	red wine vinegar	25 mL
2 tbsp	capers	25 mL
4	anchovy fillets, minced	4
½ cup	olive oil	125 mL
	Salt and freshly ground pepper to taste	
¼ cup	chopped fresh basil or parsley	50 mL
1 lb	spaghetti	500 g

1. Roast or broil the peppers until charred and blackened. Cool and peel off the skins. Seed and cut the peppers into julienned strips.

2. Place the peppers and tomatoes in a large bowl. Stir in the garlic, chili flakes, olives, vinegar, capers and anchovies. Mix well. Stir in the oil and season with salt and pepper. Add the basil.

3. Cook the spaghetti *al dente*. Drain and rinse with cold water. Combine well with the dressing. Taste and adjust seasonings. Serve cold or at room temperature.

LOWER-FAT VERSION: *Use half the olives and half the olive oil.*

Fennel and Black Olive Salad

Fennel is a fabulous, slightly anise- or licorice-flavoured vegetable. I like to use it in dips, soups and salads. When it is cooked it becomes milder in flavour. This salad is also delicious when you grill the fennel slices.

SERVES 6 TO 8

DRESSING

½ cup	black olives	125 mL
1	anchovy fillet, minced	1
1	clove garlic, minced	1
1 tsp	capers, chopped	5 mL
2 tbsp	lemon juice	25 mL
½ tsp	freshly ground pepper	2 mL
⅓ cup	olive oil	75 mL
	Salt to taste	
2 tbsp	chopped fresh basil or parsley	25 mL

SALAD

2	bulbs fennel, trimmed	2
1	red onion	1
¼ cup	slivered sun-dried tomatoes (optional)	50 mL
1	head radicchio	1

1. Pit and mince 3 olives for the dressing. Reserve the remaining olives.

2. To make the dressing, combine the minced olives with all the remaining dressing ingredients using a whisk, or in a blender or food processor.

3. Slice the fennel and break apart into pieces.

4. Sliver the red onion and combine with the fennel, reserved olives and tomatoes.

5. Toss the vegetables with the dressing. Taste and adjust seasonings if necessary. Serve the salad on a bed of radicchio.

Lentil and Rice Salad

The tiny red lentils (sometimes called pink or orange lentils) disintegrate when cooked, so I like to use them in soups or stews. When I want lentils with a definite texture, I use the small green ones (sometimes called French) or the more commonly available large greeny-brown ones.

SERVES 8 TO 10

1½ cups	green lentils	375 mL
1½ cups	basmati rice	375 mL
3	red peppers (preferably roasted and peeled, see page 99), diced	3
6	green onions, chopped	6
⅓ cup	black olives, pitted	75 mL
¼ cup	red wine vinegar	50 mL
¾ cup	olive oil	175 mL
2	cloves garlic, minced	2
1	shallot, minced	1
1 tsp	Dijon mustard	5 mL
1 tsp	salt	5 mL
½ tsp	freshly ground pepper	2 mL
2 tbsp	chopped fresh basil	25 mL
2 tbsp	chopped fresh parsley	25 mL
1	bunch arugula, chopped	1

1. Rinse the lentils and discard any stones. Cover generously with water and cook for 25 to 30 minutes, or until tender. Drain well. Cool.

2. Meanwhile, place the rice in a sieve and rinse until the water runs clean. Cook in a large pot of boiling water until tender, about 10 minutes. Drain in a sieve. Rinse with cold water and drain. Cool. Combine the lentils, rice, red peppers, green onions and olives.

3. Combine the vinegar, oil, garlic, shallot, mustard, salt and pepper. Taste and adjust the seasonings if necessary.

4. Combine the dressing with the lentil mixture. Stir in the herbs and arugula.

LOWER-FAT VERSION: *Omit the olives. Use ½ cup/125 mL tomato juice and ¼ cup/50 mL olive oil in place of ¾ cup/175 mL olive oil.*

SOUTHWEST BEAN SALAD

Chipotle chiles are smoked jalapeños. They are available dried, canned and pureed. They add a fiery, smoky taste to dishes.

The corn chips are optional, but they do make unusual croutons for this salad.

SERVES 8 TO 10

I cup	dried black beans	250 mL
3	tomatoes, seeded and diced	3
2 cups	corn niblets (raw or cooked)	500 mL
½ cup	diced mild green chiles	125 mL
I cup	diced chèvre (goat cheese) or feta cheese	250 mL
⅓ cup	pine nuts, toasted	75 mL
⅓ cup	chopped fresh cilantro	75 mL
I	chipotle or jalapeño chile, minced	I
I	clove garlic, minced	I
½ tsp	ground cumin	2 mL
3 tbsp	lime juice	45 mL
½ cup	olive oil	125 mL
	Salt and freshly ground pepper to taste	
3 cups	corn chips, broken up (optional)	750 mL

1. Rinse the beans. Using the long-soak method, soak beans in plenty of cold water for 3 hours or overnight in the refrigerator. Or, use the quick soak method by covering beans with plenty of cold water and bringing to a boil. In either case, drain. Cover again with lots of water and cook gently for 1 to 2 hours, or until tender. Drain well and cool.

2. Combine the beans with the tomatoes, corn, mild chiles, chèvre, pine nuts and cilantro.

3. For the dressing, combine the chipotle, garlic and cumin. Blend in the lime juice, oil, salt and pepper.

4. Combine the dressing with the bean mixture. Taste and adjust the seasonings if necessary. Just before serving, toss in the corn chips.

LOWER-FAT VERSION: *Use half the cheese and half the nuts. Omit the corn chips. In the dressing, use ¼ cup/50 mL olive oil and ¼ cup/50 mL orange juice instead of ½ cup/125 mL olive oil.*

VINAIGRETTE

Although this is the most basic of all salad dressings, it probably is still the best. And there are many, many variations. Vinaigrettes are very easy to make, but it is important to use high-quality ingredients. When there are only a few ingredients in a recipe, the taste of each one is quite prominent.

The best olive oil for salads is extra-virgin. It is made from the first pressing of the olives, which are cold pressed. For a sweet, smooth flavour, extra-virgin olive oil also contains less than one percent acidity. The best extra-virgin oils are made from olives that have naturally less than one percent acidity. Although extra-virgin oil is more expensive, the cost is generally worth it. If you are not going to use the oil within a few months, store it in the refrigerator. It will turn slightly cloudy and thicken, but don't worry. At room temperature it will be fine again. Make sure the salad greens are dried well before adding the dressing, and do not overdress. Toss very well until the dressing coats the greens.

Vinaigrette dressings are extremely popular right now and are even used warm over grilled foods or salads.

MAKES ¾ CUP/175 ML (ENOUGH FOR SALAD FOR 8)

3 tbsp	vinegar (white or red wine, raspberry, balsamic or herb, or lemon juice)	45 mL
1 tsp	dry mustard or Dijon mustard	5 mL
1 tsp	salt	5 mL
¼ tsp	freshly ground pepper	1 mL
8 to 12 tbsp	extra-virgin olive oil or vegetable oil	125 to 175 mL

1. Place the vinegar, mustard, salt and pepper in a bowl. Add the ingredients for any of the variations below if you wish.

2. Slowly whisk in the minimum amount of oil. Taste the dressing on a leaf of lettuce. Add more oil if necessary.

3. Toss well with salad greens just before serving.

LOWER-FAT VERSION: *The sweeter the vinegar, the less oil you need to compensate for the harshness of the vinegar. Use a good-quality olive oil—a small amount will add a lot of flavour. Use fruit or vegetable juices or purees in place of some of the oil.*

GARLIC VINAIGRETTE
Add a minced garlic clove.

HERB VINAIGRETTE
Add 2 tbsp/25 mL chopped fresh chives, basil, rosemary, chervil, parsley or tarragon (or a combination).

MUSTARD VINAIGRETTE
Add 1 tbsp/15 mL Dijon mustard instead of 1 tsp/5 mL.

CREAMY VINAIGRETTE
Substitute 3 tbsp/45 mL whipping cream for 3 tbsp/45 mL oil.

Tarragon Salad Dressing

This is a creamy-style, well-seasoned dressing. It is wonderful on lettuce, spinach or tomatoes. It also makes a great sauce for cold chicken or sliced roast veal.

The oil you use is very important, as it is the major ingredient. Taste the oil before using to make sure you like it on its own. If you add too much oil to the dressing, you can always add a little more vinegar. Toss the dressing with the greens just before serving. Use only enough dressing to coat the leaves lightly—don't drown them. (Extra dressing will keep in the refrigerator for a few days.)

MAKES ¾ CUP/175 ML

2 tbsp	mayonnaise	25 mL
2 tbsp	red wine vinegar	25 mL
I tsp	dry mustard	5 mL
I tsp	salt	5 mL
¼ tsp	freshly ground pepper	I mL
I	small clove garlic, minced (optional)	I
I tsp	dried tarragon (or I tbsp/15 mL fresh)	5 mL
I tbsp	chopped fresh parsley	15 mL
⅓ cup	olive oil or vegetable oil	75 mL

1. By hand with a whisk, or in a blender or food processor, combine the mayonnaise, vinegar, mustard, salt, pepper, garlic, tarragon and parsley.

2. Very slowly, whisking constantly, add the oil. Taste the dressing on a leaf of lettuce and, if it is too tart, add more oil.

BREADS AND MUFFINS

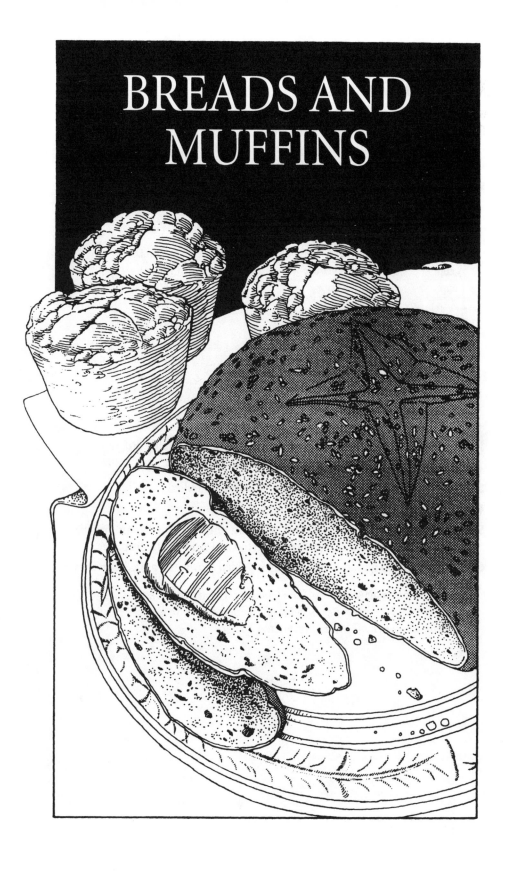

Cornbread with Cheese Custard Filling

With North American cooking becoming so popular, recipes for cornbread abound. There are many different styles of cornbread, as well as different ingredient variations and cooking methods. This one is moist and cheesy and slightly spicy because of the green chiles.

SERVES 4 TO 6

¾ cup	grated old Cheddar cheese	175 mL
I	4-oz/110 g tin mild green chiles, chopped	I
2 tbsp	chopped black olives	25 mL
⅔ cup	unflavoured yogurt	150 mL
I cup	all-purpose flour	250 mL
2 tbsp	granulated sugar	25 mL
4 tsp	baking powder	20 mL
I cup	yellow cornmeal	250 mL
½ tsp	salt	2 mL
2	eggs	2
I cup	milk	250 mL
¼ cup	unsalted butter, melted	50 mL

1. Preheat the oven to 400°F/200°C. Butter an 8-inch/1.5 L baking dish.

2. Combine the cheese with the chiles, olives and yogurt and reserve.

3. Combine the flour, sugar, baking powder, cornmeal and salt.

4. Combine the eggs, milk and melted butter.

5. Stir the egg mixture into the flour mixture just until combined. Pour into the prepared pan. Pour the cheese mixture on top and swirl it into the batter.

6. Bake for 25 to 30 minutes, until the top is golden brown and puffed. Serve warm.

LOWER-FAT VERSION: *Use half the Cheddar. Omit the olives. Use 1 egg and 2 egg whites instead of 2 whole eggs. Use low-fat milk and olive oil instead of melted butter.*

Mostly Whole Wheat Bread

If you use only whole wheat flour in bread, your bread will have a wonderful nutty flavour but may be quite dense. Therefore I usually prefer to combine whole wheat and all-purpose flour. I like the whole wheat flour for its flavour and healthful qualities and the all-purpose for its texture.

MAKES 2 LOAVES

I tbsp	granulated sugar	15 mL
½ cup	warm water	125 mL
2	packages dry yeast	2
2 cups	milk	500 mL
I tbsp	salt	15 mL
⅓ cup	honey	75 mL
2 tbsp	vegetable oil	25 mL
3 cups	all-purpose flour (more if necessary)	750 mL
3 cups	whole wheat flour	750 mL
½ cup	wheat germ	125 mL
¼ cup	bran or cracked wheat (optional)	50 mL

GLAZE

I	egg	I
I tbsp	water	15 mL

1. Dissolve the sugar in the warm water and sprinkle with the yeast. Allow to rest for 10 minutes. The yeast should bubble up and double in volume.

2. Heat the milk, salt, honey and oil until the salt has dissolved. Cool to lukewarm.

3. Combine 2 cups/500 mL of all purpose flour and 2 cups/500 mL whole wheat flour with wheat germ and bran in a large bowl.

4. Stir down the yeast. Add it to the milk mixture and combine well. Add the liquid ingredients to the flour mixture and combine well. Dough will be sticky. Add more flour until you can handle dough, but it should still be moist.

5. Sprinkle the work surface with flour and knead the dough until it is satiny, about 10 minutes. If you have a mixmaster that is strong enough for bread dough, knead for about 7 minutes.

6. Butter a large bowl and turn the dough around in it so that all sides are greasy. Cover the bowl with plastic wrap and then a tea towel. Set it in a warm place to rise until doubled in bulk, about 1½ hours.

7. Punch the dough down and divide it in half. Roll each half into a rectangle and roll up tightly to fit two 8- x 4-inch/1.5 L bread pans. Butter the pans and place the dough in them to rise a final time, about 1 hour. (The loaves should be loosely covered and in a warm place.)

8. Preheat the oven to 400°F/200°C. Combine the egg and water to make the glaze. Brush the loaves with the glaze and bake for 30 to 40 minutes. Remove the bread from the pans and cool on racks. Don't eat it all at once!

LOWER-FAT VERSION: *Use low-fat milk and half the oil.*

APRICOT ALMOND QUICKBREAD

This recipe is so easy and fast that it's hard to believe it can be so delicious. To toast the almonds, spread them on a baking sheet and bake at 350°F/180°C for 5 to 10 minutes, or until light brown. They will have much more flavour.

The easiest way to chop dried apricots is to cut them with scissors.

MAKES ONE 9- x 5-INCH/2 L LOAF

¾ cup	dried apricots	175 mL
I cup	boiling water	250 mL
2 cups	all-purpose flour	500 mL
I tbsp	baking powder	15 mL
¾ cup	granulated sugar	175 mL
½ cup	sliced almonds, preferably toasted	125 mL
2	eggs	2
I cup	milk	250 mL
⅓ cup	unsalted butter, melted	75 mL
¼ tsp	pure almond extract	I mL
½ tsp	pure vanilla extract	2 mL

1. Preheat the oven to 350°F/180°C.

2. Chop the dried apricots. Place them in a bowl and cover with the boiling water. Allow them to rest for 10 minutes while preparing the batter.

3. Combine the flour, baking powder and sugar. Stir together well. Stir in the almonds.

4. Combine the eggs, milk, melted butter and extracts. Pour the wet ingredients over the dry ingredients and stir only until blended.

5. Drain the apricots and pat dry with paper towels. Stir them into the batter. Spoon the mixture into a buttered 8- x 4-inch/1.5 L loaf pan and bake for 1 hour. Allow the loaf to rest in the pan for 10 minutes before inverting onto a wire rack to cool.

LOWER-FAT VERSION: *Use 1 whole egg plus 2 whites instead of 2 whole eggs. Use low-fat milk. Use only ¼ cup/50 mL butter.*

Apple Oatmeal Bread

One of my students, Dick Dewhurst, taught me the delicious trick of cooking oats in apple juice. It's delicious as oatmeal and also wonderful when the leftovers are made into bread. If you don't have quite enough leftover oatmeal, make up the difference with apple juice or milk. To make the cereal for the bread, cook 1 cup/250 mL oats in 2 cups/500 mL apple juice for 5 minutes.

MAKES 2 LOAVES

I tsp	granulated sugar	5 mL
½ cup	warm water	125 mL
I	package dry yeast	I
2 cups	oatmeal cooked in apple juice (or any cooked cereal), warm	500 mL
¼ cup	unsalted butter, melted, or vegetable oil	50 mL
I ½ tsp	salt	7 mL
¼ cup	brown sugar	50 mL
½ cup	bran	125 mL
I cup	whole wheat flour	250 mL
4 cups	all-purpose flour (approx.)	I L

GLAZE

I	egg	I
¼ tsp	salt	I mL

1. Dissolve the granulated sugar in the warm water and sprinkle with yeast. Allow to rest for 10 minutes, or until doubled in volume and bubbly.

2. Combine the oatmeal with the butter, salt and brown sugar. Stir to dissolve and combine the ingredients well. Stir in the dissolved yeast.

3. Combine the bran with the whole wheat flour and 2 cups/500 mL all-purpose flour. Stir in the oatmeal-yeast mixture. Add additional flour (do this by hand, in a heavy-duty mixer or a large food processor) until the dough is soft and manageable but not too sticky. (Knead for 10 minutes by hand, 5 minutes in a mixer and 1 minute in the food processor.)

4. Place the dough in a well-buttered bowl, cover and allow to rise in a warm place for 1½ to 2 hours, or until doubled in bulk.

5. Punch the dough down and divide in two. Roll each piece into a rectangle and roll up to fit the loaf pans. Place the loaves in two 8- x 4-inch/1.5 L loaf pans that have been buttered and lined with parchment paper. Cover with buttered plastic wrap and allow to rise in a warm place for 1 to 1½ hours, until doubled.

6. Preheat the oven to 400°F/200°C.

7. Combine the egg with the salt and brush the loaves with this glaze. Bake for 35 to 45 minutes. Remove from the pans and cool on wire racks.

LOWER-FAT VERSION: *Use 2 tbsp/25 mL vegetable oil instead of ¼ cup/50 mL butter.*

BRIOCHE

Brioche is a luxurious, rich French breakfast bread. It is not at all hard to prepare (although it tastes as if it is!). It makes a great snack and is also perfect to serve for brunch. Leftovers can be used to make wonderfully rich bread puddings (see page 172), fabulous French toast and exquisite "melba"-type toast to use for hors d'oeuvre.

Classic brioche pans are the fluted ones shown below, but you can also bake the dough in loaves to use as toast or in sandwiches and canapés.

MAKES 12 SMALL LOAVES

2 tsp	granulated sugar	10 mL
½ cup	warm milk	125 mL
1	package dry yeast	1
4 cups	all-purpose flour	1 L
1½ tsp	salt	7 mL
2 tbsp	granulated sugar	25 mL
3	eggs	3
2	egg yolks	2
¾ cup	unsalted butter, at room temperature	175 mL

GLAZE

1	egg	1
½ tsp	salt	2 mL

1. Dissolve 2 tsp/10 mL sugar in the warm milk and sprinkle the yeast on top. Allow to rest for 10 minutes, or until the yeast bubbles up.

2. In a large bowl (or bowl of a mixer with a dough hook), combine 2½ cups/625 mL flour with the salt and 2 tbsp/25 mL sugar. Mix well.

3. Beat the eggs and egg yolks together. Stir down the yeast and add to the eggs. Stir the egg mixture into the flour mixture by hand or with the mixer. (The dough should be sticky.)

4. Beat in the butter and add extra flour until the dough can just be handled without sticking too much. The trick is not to add too much flour, but you must be able to knead the dough a little. If mixing by hand, knead for about 5 minutes with floured hands. In a mixer, beat for 3 to 4 minutes. Dough will be slightly sticky.

5. Place the dough in a buttered bowl (turn the dough over to coat completely with the butter), cover with plastic wrap and allow to rise for 1 hour at room temperature or until the dough has doubled in bulk.

6. Punch the dough down, knead slightly and place in the bowl again. Cover and allow to rise in the refrigerator overnight or even for a few days.

7. To shape small buns, divide the dough into 12 pieces. Break off about one-eighth of each piece for the topknot. Shape the large piece into a nice ball and place in a buttered brioche pan. Shape each small piece into a pear shape. With scissors, cut a cross into the top of each bun, as shown. Insert the pointed end of the pear piece in the slit. Push together gently. Cover loosely with buttered plastic wrap and allow to rise in a warm place for about 1½ hours, or until doubled in bulk.

8. Preheat the oven to 400°F/200°C.

9. Beat the egg and salt together and brush on top of the dough. Bake for 15 to 20 minutes. Remove from the pans and cool on racks.

LOWER-FAT VERSION: *Use low-fat milk. Use 3 whole eggs instead of 3 eggs and 2 yolks. Use half the butter.*

FOOD PROCESSOR METHOD

If you are making this in the food processor, use cold butter. Add the dry ingredients to the work bowl as in Step 2, using only 2½ cups/625 mL flour. Add the cold butter in bits to the flour and process until the butter is in tiny pieces. Beat the eggs with the yolks and yeast mixture. With the machine running, slowly drizzle the liquid ingredients into the dry ingredients. (The mixture should be quite sticky!) Add enough flour for the dough to clean the sides of the work bowl (the dough should still be moist). Process for 1 minute. Continue as in Step 5.

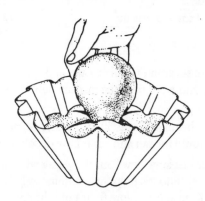

LABOUR OF LOVE STICKY BUNS

*This recipe has always had a special meaning for me. It is dedicated to
Dr. Shime at Toronto General Hospital. When I was in labour with my son,
Mark, the doctor told me to keep busy, so I made these buns. When they were
ready, I went to the hospital. My husband and Dr. Shime ate the buns for
breakfast!*

*(Note: When I was preparing this recipe, I lay down on the floor every
ten minutes and had a contraction, but if you are not in labour, this is not
necessary!)*

MAKES 15 TO 18 BUNS

DOUGH

1 tbsp	granulated sugar	15 mL
¼ cup	warm water	50 mL
1	package dry yeast	1
2 cups	milk	500 mL
¼ cup	granulated sugar	50 mL
2 tsp	salt	10 mL
¼ cup	unsalted butter	50 mL
6 cups	all-purpose flour (approx.)	1.5 L

FILLING

1 cup	unsalted butter, at room temperature (or more)	250 mL
2 cups	brown sugar (or more)	500 mL
2 tbsp	cinnamon	25 mL
½ cup	chopped toasted walnuts	125 mL
½ cup	raisins	125 mL

1. Dissolve 1 tbsp/15 mL sugar in the warm water and sprinkle dry yeast over it. Allow to rest for 10 minutes, or until the mixture bubbles up and doubles in volume.

2. Meanwhile, combine the milk, ¼ cup/50 mL sugar, salt and butter and heat until the butter melts. Stir until the salt and sugar have dissolved. Cool to lukewarm.

3. Place 4 cups/1 L flour in a large bowl. Stir the yeast and combine it with the luke-warm milk mixture. Stir into the flour and combine well. (The mixture will probably be very sticky.) Keep adding more flour until the dough can be handled. (Do not worry if you need less or more than 6 cups/1.5 L flour. The dough should be nice and soft but not so sticky that it sticks to your fingers.) Knead the dough for about 5 minutes. (This can also be done in a heavy-duty mixmaster with the dough hook, or in a large food processor with the plastic blade. Knead for 3 minutes in a mixmaster or 30 seconds in a food processor.)

4. Place the dough in a well-buttered bowl and turn so that the dough is well greased all over. Cover with plastic wrap and allow to rise in a warm, cosy spot for 1 to 1½ hours, or until doubled in bulk.

5. Punch the dough down and divide in half. Roll each half out into a large rectangle, about ¼ inch/5 mm thick. Spread each rectangle generously with butter. Then sprinkle generously with brown sugar and cinnamon.

6. Sprinkle the nuts and raisins over both halves. Roll up each rectangle lengthwise. Cut into 1½-inch/4 cm pieces.

7. Generously butter a 13- x 9-inch/3 L baking dish. Sprinkle generously with brown sugar. Arrange the rolls side by side in the dish with the spiral side facing up. Cover with buttered plastic wrap and allow to rise in a warm, cosy place for about 1 hour, or until the dough has doubled in size.

8. Preheat the oven to 400°F/200°C. Bake the buns for 30 to 40 minutes. Turn out of the pan as soon as you remove them from the oven and allow the syrup to run all over them.

LOWER-FAT VERSION: *Use low-fat milk. Use half the butter in the dough and one-third the butter in the filling. Omit the nuts.*

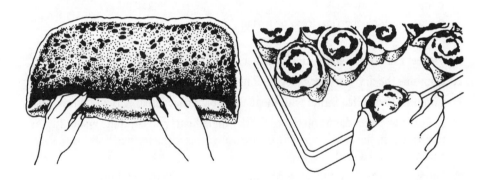

Banana Blueberry Muffins

Oat bran has been touted as one of the new healthful ingredients of our times. It is a soluble fibre that is said to help reduce blood cholesterol. It can be added to breads, muffins, hamburgers or toppings for crisps for a wonderful oat flavour.

MAKES 12 LARGE MUFFINS

2 cups	all-purpose flour	500 mL
¼ cup	oat bran	50 mL
¼ tsp	salt	1 mL
2 tsp	baking powder	10 mL
¼ tsp	baking soda	1 mL
	Grated peel of 1 orange	
½ cup	brown sugar	125 mL
⅓ cup	unsalted butter, melted	75 mL
1	small ripe banana, mashed	1
½ tsp	pure vanilla extract	2 mL
2	eggs	2
1 cup	buttermilk	250 mL
1 cup	blueberries, fresh or frozen	250 mL

1. Preheat the oven to 400°F/200°C. Butter 12 large muffin pans.

2. Combine the dry ingredients together in a bowl.

3. Combine the melted butter with the mashed banana, vanilla, eggs and buttermilk.

4. Pour the wet ingredients on top of the dry ingredients and combine just until mixed. Stir in the blueberries (if you are using frozen blueberries, make sure they have been patted dry).

5. Spoon the batter into the buttered pans and bake for 25 to 30 minutes.

LOWER-FAT VERSION: *Use one whole egg and 2 egg whites in place of the 2 whole eggs. Use half the butter. (The buttermilk is already low in fat, as unlikely as that sounds!)*

DATE AND YOGURT MUFFINS

The dates in this recipe keep the muffins very moist. Try using an ice-cream scoop to scoop muffin batter into the pans. It gives the muffins nicely rounded tops.

MAKES 12 EXTRA-LARGE MUFFINS

1 cup	dates, pitted and diced	250 mL
½ cup	chopped toasted walnuts	125 mL
2 cups	bran	500 mL
1½ cups	all-purpose flour	375 mL
1½ tsp	baking powder	7 mL
1½ tsp	baking soda	7 mL
pinch	salt	pinch
½ cup	vegetable oil	125 mL
1 cup	brown sugar	250 mL
2	eggs	2
1½ cups	unflavoured yogurt	375 mL

1. Preheat the oven to 400°F/200°C. Butter 12 extra-large muffin pans.

2. Mix the dates and nuts with the bran, flour, baking powder, baking soda and salt.

3. Combine the oil with the sugar, eggs and yogurt.

4. Stir the wet ingredients into the dry ingredients, just until blended. Scoop into muffin pans and bake for 20 to 30 minutes.

LOWER-FAT VERSION: *Use only ⅓ cup/75 mL oil. Use 1 whole egg and 2 egg whites instead of 2 whole eggs. Use low-fat yogurt. Omit walnuts or use half.*

CORNBREAD MUFFINS

Lots of restaurants are serving some form of cornbread. And why not? It only takes a minute to make and guests feel special when they are served homemade bread. This can also be baked in a 9-inch/2 L baking dish and cut into squares (bake 30 to 40 minutes until firm in the centre).

MAKES 12 MEDIUM OR 8 LARGE MUFFINS

¾ cup	yellow cornmeal	175 mL
1 cup	all-purpose flour	250 mL
¼ cup	granulated sugar	50 mL
1 tbsp	baking powder	15 mL
¼ tsp	salt	1 mL
1	egg, lightly beaten	1
1 cup	milk	250 mL
¼ cup	unsalted butter, melted	50 mL

1. Preheat the oven to 400°F/200°C. Butter the muffin pans or line with paper muffin cups.

2. Combine the cornmeal, flour, sugar, baking powder and salt. Stir well.

3. Combine the egg, milk and melted butter. Stir into the dry mixture and combine just until blended.

4. Scoop the filling into the prepared muffin pans. Bake for 20 to 25 minutes.

LOWER-FAT VERSION: *Use 2 egg whites instead of 1 whole egg. Use olive oil instead of the butter.*

ORANGE PECAN MUFFINS

The orange flavour is terrific in these delicious, healthful muffins. They are quite dense, but full of good things.

MAKES 18 MEDIUM MUFFINS

2 cups	all-purpose flour	500 mL
1 cup	wheat bran	250 mL
½ cup	oat bran	125 mL
1½ tsp	baking soda	7 mL
1½ tsp	baking powder	7 mL
½ tsp	salt	2 mL
1 tsp	cinnamon	5 mL
1 cup	brown sugar	250 mL
½ cup	unsalted butter, melted, or vegetable oil	125 mL
2	eggs	2
1¼ cups	unflavoured yogurt	300 mL
¼ cup	frozen orange juice concentrate	50 mL
2 tbsp	grated orange peel	25 mL
¾ cup	coarsely chopped toasted pecans	175 mL

1. Preheat the oven to 400°F/200°C. Butter the muffin pans well.

2. Combine the dry ingredients together in a bowl. Combine the butter, eggs, yogurt and orange juice concentrate.

3. Stir the yogurt mixture into the dry ingredients until barely blended. Quickly stir in the orange peel and nuts.

4. Spoon the batter into the prepared pans and bake for 20 to 25 minutes.

LOWER-FAT VERSION: *Use ⅓ cup/75 mL vegetable oil. Use 1 whole egg and 2 whites instead of 2 whole eggs. Use low-fat yogurt. Add only ¼ cup/50 mL pecans.*

Mini Banana Muffins

Kids love these adorable little muffins, and they are great to take to children's programs when it's your turn to make the snack. They are so easy that the kids can help make them. And they freeze well, so you can just defrost what you need.

Use the mini muffin tins or even just aluminum foil cups that are approximately 1½ inches/4 cm in diameter.

For a more sophisticated dessert, hollow out the centre of the muffins with a melon baller and pipe chocolate icing (see page 144) or partially set chocolate mousse (see page 166) into the hollows. Top with a banana chip.

MAKES 3 DOZEN MINI MUFFINS

2 cups	all-purpose flour	500 mL
¼ tsp	salt	1 mL
2 tsp	baking powder	10 mL
¼ tsp	baking soda	1 mL
½ cup	granulated sugar	125 mL
⅓ cup	unsalted butter, melted	75 mL
1	small ripe banana, mashed	1
½ tsp	pure vanilla extract	2 mL
2	eggs	2
1 cup	unflavoured yogurt	250 mL
½ cup	chocolate chips (optional)	125 mL

1. Preheat the oven to 400°F/200°C. Butter 36 mini muffin cups or use mini foil cups.

2. Combine the dry ingredients together in a bowl.

3. Combine the melted butter with the mashed banana, vanilla, eggs and yogurt.

4. Pour the wet ingredients on top of the dry ingredients and combine only until mixed. Stir in the chocolate chips if you are using them.

5. Spoon the batter into the pans and bake for 10 to 15 minutes.

LOWER-FAT VERSION: *Use only ¼ cup/50 mL butter. Use 1 whole egg and 2 whites instead of 2 whole eggs. Use low-fat yogurt or buttermilk. Omit the chocolate chips.*

CAKES

MOCHA TRIFLE CAKE

Many traditional Italian meals are completed with fruit and cheese. But there are some spectacular Italian desserts served on special occasions. This is one of them. This cake freezes well, but I like to decorate it with the cream just before serving. If you don't care about the "bomba" shape, simply assemble the layers in a regular round or square cake shape.

SERVES 12

1	sponge cake (see page 140), baked in three 9-inch/23 cm layer pans or one 9-inch/23 cm springform pan and cut horizontally into three layers	1
½ cup	rum	125 mL
FILLING		
1 cup	unsalted butter	250 mL
2 cups	sifted icing sugar	500 mL
⅓ cup	extra-strong coffee	75 mL
1 tbsp	Amaretto	15 mL
¾ cup	chopped bittersweet or semisweet chocolate	175 mL
1 cup	chopped toasted almonds	250 mL
ICING		
1½ cups	whipping cream	375 mL
3 tbsp	icing sugar, sifted	45 mL
1 tbsp	rum	15 mL
1 tbsp	Amaretto	15 mL
1 tbsp	cocoa	15 mL

1. Cut one layer of sponge cake into eight wedges. Line a bomba-shaped 4-qt/4 L mixing bowl (about 9 inches/23 cm in diameter) with plastic wrap, as shown. Cut one of the remaining cake layers to fit into the bottom of the bowl. Reserve the scraps. Wedge the eight wedges up the sides. (Do not worry if it is not perfect because the whole thing will eventually be iced.) Sprinkle the cake with rum.

2. For the filling, beat the butter until it is light and fluffy. Gradually beat in the icing sugar and continue beating until very light. Add the coffee and Amaretto, and then fold in the chocolate and nuts.

3. Spoon half the filling into the cake-lined bowl. Arrange the extra scraps of cake (from the second layer) on top. Sprinkle with rum. Cover with the remaining filling and then top with the third cake layer, which should just cover everything nicely. Sprinkle with the remaining rum. Cover with plastic wrap and refrigerate overnight.

4. To make the icing, whip the cream until light. Beat in the icing sugar and the liqueurs.

5. Line a serving plate with strips of waxed paper. Unwrap the bomba and unmould. Spread some cream over the bomba. Use the remaining cream to pipe over the cake. Dust with cocoa. Remove the waxed paper and refrigerate until ready to serve.

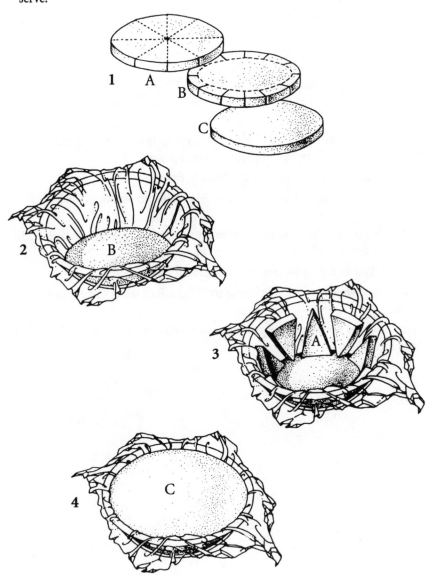

ALL-PURPOSE SPONGE CAKE

This is a delicious sponge cake that can be used for trifle (see page 165), cakes (see page 138) or whenever you want a plain, light, but really good cake (sponge cakes are also low in fat). It can also be baked as a jelly roll, but reduce the baking time to 20 to 25 minutes.

MAKES ONE ROUND 9-INCH/23 CM SPRINGFORM CAKE

I cup	cake and pastry flour	250 mL
¼ tsp	baking powder	I mL
pinch	salt	pinch
3	eggs, separated	3
⅓ cup	ice water	75 mL
I cup	granulated sugar	250 mL
¼ tsp	pure almond extract	I mL
½ tsp	pure vanilla extract	2 mL
¼ tsp	cream of tartar	I mL

1. Preheat the oven to 325°F/160°C. Line an ungreased 9-inch/23 cm springform pan with a round of parchment paper or waxed paper.

2. Sift together the flour, baking powder and salt. Reserve.

3. Beat the egg yolks until thick and lemony. Beat in the ice water until pale and foamy.

4. Add the sugar and beat until the mixture is very light and the sugar is dissolved, about 10 minutes with an electric beater. Add the extracts.

5. Fold the flour into the yolk mixture in three additions.

6. Beat the egg whites and cream of tartar until light. Fold the egg whites into the batter.

7. Turn the batter gently into the pan and bake for 40 to 50 minutes. Cool on a rack before removing from the pan.

PEACH UPSIDE-DOWN CAKE

This is an old-fashioned, friendly dessert. And easy (you don't even have to peel the peaches if you don't want to)! The recipe also works well with plums or sliced pineapple.

MAKES ONE 8-INCH/20 CM SQUARE CAKE

BASE

¼ cup	unsalted butter	50 mL
I cup	firmly packed brown sugar	250 mL
3	medium peaches	3

CAKE

½ cup	unsalted butter, melted	125 mL
½ cup	milk	125 mL
I	egg	I
I tsp	pure vanilla extract	5 mL
½ tsp	cinnamon	2 mL
pinch	nutmeg	pinch
1½ cups	all-purpose flour	375 mL
½ cup	granulated sugar	125 mL
2 tsp	baking powder	10 mL
pinch	salt	pinch

1. Preheat the oven to 400°F/200°C.

2. To make the base, place ¼ cup/50 mL butter in an 8-inch/20 cm square baking pan and place in the oven for 5 minutes, or until melted. Add the brown sugar, stir and return to the oven until the sugar melts, about another 5 minutes.

3. Meanwhile, peel and slice the peaches. Arrange on top of the brown-sugar mixture. Add any juices accumulated while handling the peaches.

4. To make the cake, combine the melted butter, milk and egg. Add the vanilla, cinnamon and nutmeg.

5. Sift the dry ingredients together. Add the milk mixture to the flour mixture and stir only until barely combined.

6. Spread the cake batter over the peaches. Bake for 35 minutes. Allow the cake to rest for 5 minutes. Invert onto a serving plate. Serve warm or cold.

LOWER-FAT VERSION: *Use half the butter in the base. Use only ⅓ cup/75 mL butter in the cake. Use low-fat milk. Use 2 egg whites in place of 1 whole egg.*

FRUITCAKE WITH AMARETTO

Linda Stephen, who has taught many wonderful classes at my school, developed this recipe for our Gifts from the Kitchen course, and it has more or less become "fruitcake update" for most of my students. Even people who don't normally like fruitcake will love this recipe.

If you prefer a more traditionally flavoured fruitcake, add 1 tsp/5 mL cinnamon, 1 tsp/5 mL allspice, ½ tsp/2 mL nutmeg and ½ tsp/2 mL cloves to the flour.

MAKES 6 TO 7 SMALL LOAF CAKES 5½ x 3 INCHES/250 ML

⅓ cup	Amaretto	75 mL
¼ cup	golden raisins	50 mL
¼ cup	dark raisins	50 mL
1 lb	unsalted butter	500 g
2¼ cups	granulated sugar	550 mL
7	eggs	7
½ tsp	pure almond extract	2 mL
3½ cups	all-purpose flour	875 mL
½ tsp	salt	2 mL
1 tbsp	grated lemon peel	15 mL
1 tbsp	grated orange peel	15 mL
¾ cup	diced dried apricots (approx. 4 oz/125 g)	175 mL
1¼ cups	mixed candied peel (approx. 8 oz/250 g)	300 mL
⅓ cup	candied citron (approx. 2 oz/60 g)	75 mL
¾ cup	grated bittersweet or semisweet chocolate (approx. 4 oz/125 g)	175 mL

1. Pour the Amaretto over both kinds of raisins and allow to rest for 1 hour. Butter the loaf pans, line with parchment paper and butter again.

2. Preheat the oven to 325°F/160°C.

3. Beat the butter until light. Gradually beat in the sugar. Add the eggs, two at a time, beating well after each addition. Add the almond extract with the last egg.

4. Combine the flour with the salt and stir into the batter. Do not overmix. Mix in the raisins and all the remaining ingredients.

5. Spoon the batter into the prepared pans. Bake for 50 minutes, or until a cake tester inserted in the centre of a loaf comes out clean.

6. Allow the cakes to cool for 15 minutes in the pans before unmoulding. Cool completely on racks. Wrap in foil and store in the refrigerator.

RAY'S SQUARE APPLE PIE CAKE

My husband loves apples, and he is always trying to get me to recreate his favourite childhood dessert. His clues are "It's not really a pie, it's not really a cake, it's not really a crisp." I have not been successful yet, but he loves me more each time I try. "This version is getting close," he says.

SERVES 8 TO 10

CRUST

2 cups	all-purpose flour	500 mL
2 tbsp	granulated sugar	25 mL
pinch	salt	pinch
¾ cup	unsalted butter, cold	175 mL
1	egg, cold, lightly beaten	1
2 tbsp	ice water	25 mL

FILLING

6	apples (Spy or Golden Delicious)	6
⅓ cup	all-purpose flour	75 mL
⅓ cup	brown sugar	75 mL
½ tsp	cinnamon	2 mL
2 tbsp	unsalted butter, cold, cut into bits	25 mL

GLAZE

1	egg	1
1 tbsp	granulated sugar	15 mL

1. To make the crust, combine 2 cups/500 mL flour with 2 tbsp/25 mL granulated sugar and salt. Cut ¾ cup/175 mL butter into small pieces and cut into the flour until the mixture resembles fresh breadcrumbs.

2. Beat the egg with the water and add to the flour. Gather the dough together to form a ball. Wrap and refrigerate while preparing the filling.

3. To make the filling, peel the apples, cut them in half and remove the cores. Slice or dice and place in a large bowl. Combine ⅓ cup/75 mL flour, brown sugar, cinnamon and 2 tbsp/25 mL butter and combine well with the apples. Reserve.

4. Preheat the oven to 400°F/200°C. Divide the dough in half. Roll out one piece to fit the bottom of a 13- x 9-inch/3 L baking pan. Press or roll the dough into the bottom. Spread the apples on top. Roll out the remaining dough and fit over the top. Pierce with a fork.

5. To make the glaze, beat the egg lightly and brush over the top crust. Sprinkle with 1 tbsp/15 mL granulated sugar. Bake for 1 hour. (Check after 30 minutes, and if the top crust is browning too much, reduce the heat to 350°F/180°C.)

ANNA BANANA'S BIRTHDAY CAKE
(BANANA CAKE WITH CHOCOLATE FUDGE ICING)

Everyone calls my daughter Anna Banana, and she happens to adore bananas! Therefore it was only natural to have a banana theme party for her first birthday. Everyone dressed in yellow, we had a clown dressed as a banana as entertainment, the food and table settings were all banana related or yellow, and we gave yellow loot bags that all had bananas in them. I made this cake in the shape of a heart. I wrote Happy Birthday in bright yellow on the chocolate fudge icing and made little marzipan bananas for decorations. It really was sweet, just like her.

MAKES ONE 9-INCH/23 CM CAKE

CAKE

½ cup	unsalted butter	125 mL
¾ cup	granulated sugar	175 mL
2	eggs	2
1 tsp	pure vanilla extract	5 mL
3	ripe bananas, mashed	3
2 cups	all-purpose flour	500 mL
1 tsp	baking soda	5 mL
¼ cup	sour cream	50 mL

CHOCOLATE FUDGE ICING

4 oz	bittersweet or semisweet chocolate	125 g
2 tbsp	cocoa	25 mL
⅓ cup	milk	75 mL
¼ cup	unsalted butter	50 mL
1½ cups	icing sugar, sifted (more if needed)	375 mL
1 tsp	pure vanilla extract	5 mL

1. Preheat the oven to 350°F/180°C. Butter a 9-inch/23 cm springform pan (or heart-shaped pan).

2. Cream ½ cup/125 mL butter until light. Gradually beat in the granulated sugar.

3. Add the eggs one at a time and beat after each addition. Beat in 1 tsp/5 mL vanilla and the mashed bananas.

4. Sift or mix together the dry ingredients and add to the batter alternately with the sour cream. Spoon the batter into the prepared pan evenly and bake for 30 to 40 minutes, or until the cake springs back when gently pressed in the centre. Cool for 10 minutes and invert. Cool on a wire rack.

5. For the icing, melt the chocolate, cocoa, milk and ¼ cup/50 mL butter in the top of a double boiler. Cook until smooth and cool slightly.

6. Beat in the icing sugar and 1 tsp/15 mL vanilla. Place the bowl over a larger bowl of ice and water and stir until the icing is spreadable.

7. Ice the cake and decorate as you wish.

MUD CAKE WITH FUDGE GLAZE

Everyone loves a good chocolate cake. This one is fudgy and rich, and it's baked in a tube pan for a slightly different look.

MAKES I LARGE TUBE CAKE

CAKE

1¼ cups	all-purpose flour	300 mL
1 tsp	baking powder	5 mL
½ tsp	baking soda	2 mL
pinch	salt	pinch
2 oz	unsweetened chocolate, chopped	60 g
3 tbsp	cocoa	45 mL
½ cup	boiling water	125 mL
½ cup	unsalted butter, at room temperature	125 mL
1 cup	granulated sugar	250 mL
2	eggs	2
½ tsp	pure vanilla extract	2 mL
½ cup	sour cream	125 mL

FUDGE GLAZE

6 oz	bittersweet chocolate	175 g
⅓ cup	whipping cream	75 mL
¼ cup	unsalted butter, at room temperature	50 mL
1¼ cups	icing sugar, sifted	300 mL

1. Preheat the oven to 350°F/180°C. Butter a large 10-cup/2.5 L tube pan.

2. To make the cake, sift together the flour, baking powder, baking soda and salt. Reserve.

3. Place the chopped chocolate and cocoa in a bowl. Pour the boiling water over and allow the chocolate to sit for about 2 minutes. Stir to complete the melting.

4. Cream the butter until light. Add the granulated sugar gradually and beat until light.

5. Add the eggs one at a time and beat after each addition. Blend in the chocolate, vanilla and sour cream.

6. Add the dry ingredients and blend together briefly just until combined.

7. Transfer the batter to the prepared pan and bake for 35 to 40 minutes. Do not overbake. Cool for 10 minutes in the pan and then invert onto a rack. Cool.

8. To prepare the glaze, place the chocolate, cocoa and cream in the top of a double boiler over simmering water and cook until melted and smooth. Remove from heat.

9. Beat in the butter and icing sugar and blend until smooth. Pour the glaze over the cake. (If the glaze is too thick to pour, just put it back over the boiling water until it is of pouring consistency.)

MINI CARROT CAKES WITH CREAM CHEESE ICING

These mini carrot cakes are easy to eat, and they look great and taste delicious. You can freeze individual squares—they are great to have on hand. Ice them with the cream cheese icing and decorate with toasted coconut, or make little marzipan carrots for the top. Just buy marzipan and mix batches with green and orange food colouring. Roll tiny carrot shapes with your fingers and top with green leaf shapes.

MAKES APPROX. 5 DOZEN SQUARES

½ cup	chopped toasted walnuts	125 mL
⅓ cup	unsweetened grated coconut	75 mL
½ cup	raisins	125 mL
2	large carrots, grated	2
1¾ cups	all-purpose flour	425 mL
pinch	salt	pinch
1½ tsp	baking powder	7 mL
½ tsp	baking soda	2 mL
1½ tsp	cinnamon	7 mL
¼ tsp	nutmeg	1 mL
pinch	allspice	pinch
3	eggs	3
¾ cup	brown sugar	175 mL
½ cup	granulated sugar	125 mL
¾ cup	vegetable oil	175 mL

CREAM CHEESE ICING

6 oz	cream cheese, at room temperature	175 g
¼ cup	unsalted butter, at room temperature	50 mL
1 tsp	pure vanilla extract	5 mL
3 cups	icing sugar, sifted	750 mL

1. Preheat the oven to 325°F/160°C. Butter a 12- x 18-inch/30 x 45 cm baking pan and line with parchment paper.

2. Combine the walnuts, coconut, raisins and carrots. Reserve.

3. Sift together the flour, salt, baking powder, baking soda, cinnamon, nutmeg and allspice. Reserve.

4. Beat the eggs and gradually add the sugars. Slowly add the oil, beating constantly.

5. Add the dry ingredients to the egg mixture all at once. Blend in as quickly as possible. Stir in the nut-carrot mixture.

6. Pour the batter into the prepared pan and bake for 30 to 35 minutes, or until the cake springs back when touched gently in the centre. Cool for 15 minutes and invert.

7. To make the icing, beat the cream cheese until smooth and light. Beat in the butter until well blended.

8. Blend in the vanilla. Add the icing sugar 1 cup/250 mL at a time and blend in until the icing is light and spreadable (you may need more or less icing sugar).

9. Ice the cake with the cream cheese icing. Cut the cake into 2-inch/5 cm squares and place each square in a foil cup.

Maureen's Hamburger Cake

This cake is wonderful for both children and adults. It was first made for me by Maureen Lollar, who has worked for me for many years. She has a wonderful sense of humour—as shown by this cake! Because some of the icing is butterscotch and some is chocolate, the finished cake looks just like a hamburger, complete with strawberry jam "ketchup" and sesame seeds on top.

MAKES ONE LARGE CAKE

3 oz	unsweetened chocolate	90 g
I cup	boiling water	250 mL
I tsp	baking soda	5 mL
2¼ cups	cake and pastry flour	550 mL
½ tsp	salt	2 mL
2½ tsp	baking powder	12 mL
½ cup	unsalted butter, at room temperature	125 mL
2½ cups	granulated sugar	625 mL
3	eggs, separated	3
I tsp	pure vanilla extract	5 mL
I cup	sour cream	250 mL

ICING

I¼ cups	unsalted butter	300 mL
2 cups	brown sugar	500 mL
½ cup	milk	125 mL
4 cups	icing sugar, sifted	I L
2 tbsp	cocoa	25 mL

GARNISH

I cup	strawberry jam or preserves	250 mL
I tbsp	toasted sesame seeds	15 mL

1. Preheat the oven to 350°F/180°C. Butter an 8- or 9-inch/20 or 23 cm round cake pan and line the bottom with parchment paper or waxed paper. Butter an 8- or 9-inch/20 or 23 cm round-bottomed Pyrex casserole bowl and line the bottom with paper.

2. To make the cake, combine the chocolate and water in the top of a double boiler. Heat over gently simmering water until melted. Stir well and cool slightly. Add the baking soda.

3. Sift together the flour, salt and baking powder and reserve.

4. Cream the butter until light. Gradually beat in 2 cups/500 mL granulated sugar. Add the egg yolks, one at a time, and then add the vanilla.

5. Add the chocolate mixture to the egg-yolk mixture. Add the dry ingredients alternately with the sour cream, mixing just until the ingredients are blended.

6. Beat the egg whites until light and gradually beat in the remaining ½ cup/125 mL granulated sugar. Fold the whites gently but thoroughly into the batter.

7. Pour the batter into the round cake pan until it is three-quarters full. Pour the remaining batter into the Pyrex casserole bowl. Bake for 40 to 50 minutes, or until the cakes feel firm when gently pressed at the top. Let the cakes cool for 10 minutes and then remove from the pans. Cool on racks.

8. Meanwhile, prepare the icing. Melt the butter in a saucepan. Add the brown sugar and cook for 2 minutes. Add the milk and bring to a boil. Cool.

9. Beat in the sifted icing sugar until the icing is of spreading consistency. If it is too runny, add more sugar; if it is too stiff, add 1 tbsp/15 mL boiling water. Remove ½ cup/125 mL icing and mix with the cocoa.

10. To assemble, slice the cooled cake from the round pan in two horizontally. Place one half on a cake plate. Ice the top and sides with the butterscotch icing. Place the second half on top and ice with the cocoa frosting. Spoon on the jam, allowing it to flow down the sides of the cake like ketchup. Place the large casserole-shaped cake on top with the rounded side up. Spread with butterscotch icing. Sprinkle the top with sesame seeds.

White Chocolate Lemon Mousse Cake

Rolling up a cake may sound terrifying at first, but it really does work. If you have overbaked the cake and it cracks, however, you can always put the whole thing in a trifle bowl and eat it with a spoon. (You can also bake the cake in two 9-inch/23 cm cake pans for 30 to 35 minutes. Use the white chocolate-lemon mixture as a filling and icing.)

This cake was inspired by Jim Dodge, a fabulous baker and instructor at my school.

SERVES 8 TO 10

CAKE

6	eggs	6
I cup	granulated sugar	250 mL
I tsp	pure vanilla extract	5 mL
I cup	all-purpose flour	250 mL
I tsp	grated lemon peel	5 mL

WHITE CHOCOLATE LEMON FILLING

I cup	granulated sugar	250 mL
¾ cup	lemon juice	175 mL
I tbsp	grated lemon peel	15 mL
4	eggs	4
4 oz	white chocolate, chopped	125 g
2 cups	whipping cream	500 mL

GARNISH

2 oz	white chocolate, in curls or grated	60 g
	Sprigs of fresh mint	
	Sifted icing sugar	

1. Preheat the oven to 375°F/190°C. For the cake, beat the eggs with the sugar over warm water until the sugar dissolves. Add the vanilla and whip until the eggs are very light.

2. Sift the flour over the egg mixture. Fold in gently along with the lemon peel. Spread the batter over a 17- x 11-inch/45 x 29 cm jelly roll pan lined with parchment paper that has been buttered and dusted with flour. Bake for 10 to 12 minutes. Allow to cool for 10 minutes and dust with icing sugar. Turn out of pan onto a tea towel. Remove parchment paper and roll up lengthwise to set shape. Roll up in a tea towel.

3. For the filling, heat the sugar, lemon juice and peel. Beat the eggs and mix in the hot liquid. Return to the heat and cook until the mixture just comes to a boil and thickens.

4. Add the chopped chocolate and stir until smooth. Transfer to a bowl and cool over a bowl of ice, stirring often.

5. Whip the cream until light. Fold into the chocolate base. Refrigerate for 1 hour.

6. Unroll the cake. Spread with most of the filling. Roll up again and carefully transfer to a serving platter. Pipe some reserved mousse down the centre of the cake. Sprinkle with white chocolate and garnish with mint. Dust with icing sugar.

COOKIES AND CHOCOLATES

THE SHORTEST SHORTBREAD

These are the cookies that we give out as special gifts at Christmas time. One year when Sadie Darby was the manager of my cookware shop, she took one hundred boxes home in her car to deliver the next day. Thieves, spying these valuable-looking packages, broke into her car and started down the street with them. Neighbourhood Watch saved the day and chased the thieves, whereupon the culprits dropped everything and ran. Fortunately, we only lost a few dozen in breakage, and we got to eat the broken cookies. After all, they're all the same once they're in your stomach!

I rarely use salted butter, but the flavour of these cookies are better with it. If you can't find rice flour in your supermarket, try a health-food or bulk-food store. Fruit sugar is sometimes called castor sugar, bar sugar or instant dissolving sugar. It is not icing sugar (also called powdered sugar or confectioner's sugar). It is usually available at supermarkets, but if you can't find it, just process 2 cups/500 mL regular granulated sugar in a blender or food processor for 60 to 90 seconds. Remeasure the sugar after processing.

Be careful in measuring flour in this recipe as too much will result in dry cookies. Always measure flour by lightly dipping a dry measure cup into the flour container and sweeping excess flour off the top with a straight-edge knife rather than shaking it down.

MAKES APPROX. 7 DOZEN COOKIES

I lb	salted butter, at room temperature	500 g
I cup	fruit sugar	250 mL
3½ cups	all-purpose flour	875 mL
½ cup	rice flour	125 mL

1. Preheat the oven to 300°F/150°C. Butter the cookie sheets or line them with parchment paper.

2. Cream the butter until light. Gradually beat in the sugar.

3. Combine the flours and add to the butter-sugar mixture.

4. The dough can be patted into the cookie sheets, pricked with a fork, baked and then cut into pieces. Or it can be rolled out and cut with cookie cutters; or it can be formed into balls and pressed down with a fork, glass or potato masher for a more interesting design. Bake for 25 to 35 minutes, until just barely golden.

Passover Brownies

These brownies from Marian Ash in Winnipeg are now a Passover tradition in our house in Toronto. They defy the definition of Passover baking which can sometimes be dry. They freeze perfectly and taste great with or without the glaze.

Cake meal can be found in any Jewish food store, or in some supermarkets before Passover. Many people make these brownies all year-round and love them the best.

MAKES APPROX. 2 DOZEN BROWNIES

1 ¼ cups	granulated sugar	300 mL
⅓ cup	cocoa	75 mL
½ cup	unsalted butter, melted or vegetable oil	125 mL
4	eggs	4
½ cup	cake meal	125 mL
½ cup	chopped toasted walnuts	125 mL
GLAZE		
6 oz	bittersweet or semisweet chocolate, coarsely chopped	175 g
⅓ cup	unsalted butter, or vegetable oil	75 mL

1. Preheat the oven to 350°F/180°C. Blend together the sugar and cocoa.

2. With a whisk, mix together the butter, sugar-cocoa mixture and eggs. Do not overbeat.

3. Fold in the cake meal and nuts. Pour into a lightly buttered 8-inch/2 L square baking dish. Bake for 25 minutes (do not overbake). Cool.

4. For the glaze, melt the chocolate gently with the butter and stir until smooth. Spread over the base. Refrigerate. Cut into squares.

SARAH BAND'S LEMON SQUARES

Sarah Band was a Cordon Bleu caterer before she opened her fabulous shops in Toronto. These lemon squares are a real treat.

MAKES 16 SQUARES

BASE

½ cup	unsalted butter	125 mL
2 tbsp	brown sugar	25 mL
1 cup	all-purpose flour	250 mL
pinch	salt	pinch

FILLING

2	eggs	2
1 cup	granulated sugar	250 mL
2 tsp	all-purpose flour	10 mL
1½ cups	unsweetened grated coconut	375 mL
3 tbsp	Juice and finely grated peel of 1 lemon	45 mL

ICING

¼ cup	unsalted butter	50 mL
	Juice of 1 lemon	
¾ cup	icing sugar or more (approx.)	175 mL

1. Preheat the oven to 350°F/180°C.

2. To make the base, cream ½ cup/125 mL butter with the brown sugar. Add 1 cup/250 mL flour and the salt. Press into the bottom of an 8-inch/1.5 L buttered baking dish. Bake for 10 minutes.

3. To make the filling, combine the eggs with the granulated sugar, 2 tsp/10 mL flour, coconut, juice and peel of one lemon. Pour the filling over the base and bake for 20 minutes. Cool completely.

4. To make the icing, cream ¼ cup/50 mL butter and add the lemon juice. Add enough icing sugar to make a spreadable icing. Spread over the filling. Cut into 16 squares.

CHOCOLATE BLIZZARD COOKIES

These cookies are so delicious that you have to hide them from yourself so you won't eat them all at once! The white chocolate "chips" are a wonderful change but, of course, if you do not like change, just use bittersweet or semisweet chips and call these Chocolate Tornado Cookies.

You don't have to bake these cookies all at once. They are very rich, so just cut off what you need for baking. They also freeze well after they are baked.

MAKES APPROX. 3 DOZEN COOKIES

1 lb	bittersweet or semisweet chocolate, chopped	500 g
¼ cup	unsalted butter	50 mL
½ cup	all-purpose flour	125 mL
½ tsp	baking powder	2 mL
¼ tsp	salt	1 mL
4	eggs	4
¾ cup	brown sugar	175 mL
¾ cup	granulated sugar	175 mL
10 oz	white chocolate, chopped	300 g
2 cups	chopped toasted pecans	500 mL

1. Melt the chocolate and butter over hot water. Cool slightly.

2. Sift together the flour, baking powder and salt. Reserve.

3. Beat the eggs with the sugars until light and stir in the melted chocolate. Add the flour mixture, chopped white chocolate and nuts. Refrigerate the dough until it is cold enough to mould.

4. Shape the dough into two flat rolls about 3 inches/7.5 cm in diameter, like refrigerator cookies. Roll in additional flour and wrap well in waxed paper. (Don't worry about the floury edges of the cookies after they are baked. It makes them look more blizzardy!) Freeze for 1 hour.

5. Preheat the oven to 350°F/180°C. Line cookie sheets with parchment paper. Slice the cookies ½ inch/1 cm thick. Bake only 10 to 12 minutes, or just until they lose their sheen. They should just barely hold their shape when cool, and should be moist and chewy inside. Gently lift the cookies off the cookie sheets and cool on racks.

Rugalahs (Cinnamon Crescents)

This is probably my students' all-time favourite recipe. People used to leave the class and head straight for the closest convenience store to buy the ingredients. If they could have made them in the car on the way home, they would have!

MAKES 2 DOZEN CRESCENTS

½ cup	unsalted butter, cold, cut into pieces	125 mL
I cup	all-purpose flour	250 mL
4 oz	cream cheese, cold, cut into pieces	125 g
¼ cup	brown sugar	50 mL
⅓ cup	finely chopped pecans	75 mL
I tbsp	cinnamon	15 mL
I tbsp	cocoa	15 mL
I tsp	finely grated orange peel (optional)	5 mL
½ cup	raspberry jam	125 mL

GLAZE

I	egg	I
2 tbsp	cream	25 mL
⅓ cup	granulated sugar, preferably coarse, or chopped nuts	75 mL

1. Make the pastry by cutting the butter into the flour until crumbly. Then cut in the cheese until crumbly. Gather the dough together and form a ball. Knead a few times. Divide the dough in half and shape into two balls. Wrap and refrigerate until ready to use. (The pastry can be easily made in a food processor—process until the dough just comes together.)

2. Prepare the filling by combining the brown sugar, nuts, cinnamon, cocoa and orange peel.

3. Preheat the oven to 350°F/180°C.

4. Roll out each ball of dough into a circle. The thinner the pastry, the crisper the cookies will be. Spread each round with a thin layer of jam. Sprinkle with the filling and pat it in firmly.

5. Cut each circle into 12 wedges and roll each wedge up tightly from the outside edge, as shown.

6. Butter a cookie sheet well or line with parchment paper. Arrange the crescents on the cookie sheet. Combine the egg and cream. Brush the cookies with the glaze and sprinkle with sugar. (Crescents can now be frozen.)

7. Bake for 20 to 25 minutes until golden. (Frozen crescents will require a slightly longer baking time.)

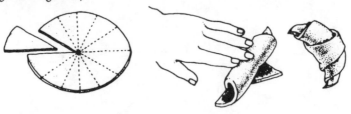

CHOCOLATE CHIP OATMEAL COOKIES

If you like cookies chewy, do not bake these too long. If you want them crisp, bake a little longer. (The first batch is usually experimental.)

MAKES 4 DOZEN COOKIES

¾ cup	unsalted butter, at room temperature	175 mL
1¼ cups	brown sugar	300 mL
1	egg	1
¼ cup	orange juice	50 mL
1 tsp	pure vanilla extract	5 mL
Pinch	salt	Pinch
¼ tsp	baking soda	1 mL
1 cup	all-purpose flour	250 mL
3 cups	rolled oats	750 mL
1 cup	chocolate chips	250 mL

1. Preheat the oven to 350°F/180°C. Butter the cookie sheets or line with parchment paper.

2. Cream the butter until light. Gradually beat in the sugar. Add the egg, orange juice and vanilla and beat well.

3. Sift or mix together the salt, baking soda and flour. Stir into the batter. Add the rolled oats and chocolate chips.

4. Use about 1 tbsp/15 mL batter for each cookie and flatten. Bake for 10 to 12 minutes. Cool on racks.

PRETZEL COOKIES

Kids seem to love things that look like something else. So these pretzel cookies usually are a big hit. Use coarse sugar to resemble the salt.

You can also use this dough for rolled cookies and cut them with cookie cutters. Chill the dough until it is easy to roll. Cut into shapes, brush with the egg, sprinkle with sugar and bake for 8 to 10 minutes (the rolled cookies are thinner than the pretzels and will take less time to bake).

MAKES 5 DOZEN COOKIES

I cup	unsalted butter, at room temperature	250 mL
I½ cups	granulated sugar	375 mL
2	eggs	2
I tsp	pure vanilla extract	5 mL
3 cups	all-purpose flour	750 mL

TOPPING

I	egg	I
½ cup	coarse granulated sugar or demerara sugar	125 mL

1. Preheat the oven to 375°F/190°C. Butter the cookie sheets or line with parchment paper.

2. Beat the butter until light. Slowly beat in the sugar. Add the eggs one at a time and beat well. Add the vanilla.

3. Stir in the flour. If the dough is too soft to handle, refrigerate it until it can be rolled and shaped.

4. Use about 2 tbsp/25 mL dough for each cookie. Roll the dough into a long strip. Make a circle with ties overlapping and then twist once. Turn the twisted end over the circle to form a pretzel, as shown.

5. Arrange the pretzels on the cookie sheets. Beat the egg and brush on top of the cookies. Sprinkle with sugar. Bake for 12 to 15 minutes (or longer) until golden.

 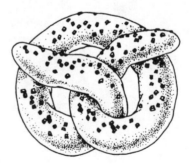

CHOCOLATE CHIP COOKIES

Chocolate chip cookies can be plain or fancy, but they are always popular. You can use chocolate chips or, for a more sophisticated version, chop up European bittersweet chocolate and use that instead. Chopped toasted pecans are also a fabulous addition, but they are optional—many children are allergic to or do not like nuts. (In fact, some children are also allergic to chocolate—use carob chips instead.)

MAKES 4 DOZEN COOKIES

I cup	unsalted butter, at room temperature	250 mL
½ cup	brown sugar	125 mL
½ cup	granulated sugar	125 mL
I tsp	pure vanilla extract	5 mL
I	egg	I
2 cups	all-purpose flour	500 mL
¼ tsp	salt	I mL
I tsp	baking soda	5 mL
I cup	chocolate chips	250 mL
I cup	chopped toasted pecans (optional)	250 mL

1. Butter the cookie sheets or line them with parchment paper.

2. Cream the butter with the sugars until light. Add the vanilla and egg and beat well.

3. Sift the flour with the salt and baking soda and add to the batter. Stir in the chocolate chips and nuts. Refrigerate the batter for 1 to 2 hours.

4. Preheat the oven to 375°F/190°C. Shape the cookies into balls about 1½ inches/ 4 cm in diameter and arrange on cookie sheets. Press down slightly.

5. Bake for 8 to 10 minutes. The longer the cookies bake, the crisper they will be. The less they bake, the chewier.

STAINED-GLASS COOKIES

These cookies are so adorable and delicious that they are worth the time and effort it takes to make them. They can be used as Christmas tree decorations, you can make a mobile with them, they are great for parties and party favours and children can even wear them as jewellery!

MAKES 4 DOZEN LARGE COOKIES

I cup	unsalted butter, at room temperature	250 mL
I ¼ cups	granulated sugar	300 mL
¼ cup	water	50 mL
3 cups	all-purpose flour	750 mL
½ tsp	baking soda	2 mL
¼ tsp	salt	I mL
5	25-g packages Lifesavers, different colours	5

1. Beat the butter until light and slowly add the sugar. Add the water and stir until smooth.

2. Sift or mix the flour with the baking soda and salt. Stir into the butter mixture. Knead it together well. (If the dough is very dry, add a little more water.)

3. Wrap in plastic wrap and chill for 30 minutes.

4. Preheat the oven to 350°F/180°C. Line cookie sheets with parchment paper.

5. Roll pieces of dough into long ropes about ½ inch/1 cm thick. Form the ropes into shapes, such as fish, boats, windows, houses, Christmas trees, etc. Press any pieces that touch each other together so that they do not separate while baking. Bake for 5 minutes.

6. Meanwhile, crush the Lifesavers, keeping each colour separate.

7. Fill in the holes between the ropes with different colours of candy. Bake for 5 to 6 minutes longer, or until the candy melts. Cool.

CHOCOLATE TRUFFLES WITH GRAND MARNIER

These are what chocoholics' dreams are made of!

I always use the best-quality chocolate I can find. If you're going to gain weight, it should be on the best food possible! Even though Swiss chocolate sounds as if it should be more expensive than domestic, it rarely is, and the flavour and texture are far superior. It does not come premeasured for you, however, and therefore a set of scales comes in handy when using it. If you are using the large 370-g Swiss chocolate bars that have 40 small squares, three little squares equals one ounce.

Bittersweet and semisweet chocolate can be used interchangeably. I like to cook with bittersweet, which usually refers to chocolate slightly less sweet than semisweet. In fact, whenever a recipe calls for semisweet or sweet chocolate, I use bittersweet. Don't confuse it with unsweetened chocolate which doesn't contain any sugar. Bittersweet chocolate is absolutely fantastic for eating while unsweetened obviously is not.

MAKES APPROX. 4 DOZEN TRUFFLES

12 oz	bittersweet or semisweet chocolate	375 g
½ cup	unsalted butter	125 mL
¼ cup	whipping cream	50 mL
2 tbsp	Grand Marnier	25 mL
1 cup	cocoa, sifted	250 mL

1. Chop the chocolate and place in the top of a double boiler over barely simmering water. Add the butter and cook, stirring, until melted together.

2. Beat in the cream and stir until smooth. Cook for 1 minute. Beat in the liqueur.

3. Transfer the mixture to a bowl. Cover. Refrigerate until firm.

4. Using a spoon or melon baller, shape the chocolate mixture into 1-inch/2.5 cm balls. Roll in cocoa.

ALMOND TRUFFLES
Add ½ cup/125 mL ground toasted almonds to the chocolate mixture and use Amaretto instead of Grand Marnier. Roll the truffles in ground toasted almonds instead of cocoa.

HAZELNUT TRUFFLES
Add ½ cup/125 mL ground toasted hazelnuts to the chocolate mixture and use Frangelico instead of Grand Marnier. Roll the truffles in ground toasted hazelnuts.

MOCHA TRUFFLES
Use 1 tbsp/15 mL dark rum and 1 tbsp/15 mL coffee liqueur instead of Grand Marnier. Roll the truffles in sifted icing sugar.

COGNAC TRUFFLES
Use Cognac instead of Grand Marnier. Roll in cocoa.

"Breakfast" Chocolate Truffles

We call these "breakfast" truffles because they contain coffee and are rolled in crushed cereal, but we hardly recommend serving them for breakfast! They freeze perfectly. You can also roll the truffles in chopped nuts, cocoa or icing sugar, but the frosted cereal is surprisingly sophisticated and delicious.

I demonstrated these for Valentine's Day on CFTO's Eye on Toronto with Robin Ward. We groaned with delight as we rolled the truffles in our chocolate-covered hands, and when Robin finished eating his truffle, he looked at me and asked, "So, Bonnie, was it as good for you as it was for me?"

MAKES APPROX. 4 DOZEN TRUFFLES

12 oz	bittersweet or semisweet chocolate, coarsely chopped	375 g
¾ cup	unsalted butter, cut in pieces	175 mL
½ cup	whipping cream	125 mL
1 tbsp	instant espresso powder	15 mL
½ tsp	pure vanilla extract	2 mL
8 oz	bittersweet or semisweet chocolate	250 g
2 cups	crushed sugar-frosted flakes	500 mL

1. Place the chopped chocolate, butter, cream and espresso powder in a saucepan. Cook on low heat until barely melted. Stir until smooth.

2. Cool over a larger bowl filled with ice and water, stirring often, until the mixture thickens.

3. On a baking sheet lined with waxed paper, pipe or spoon the mixture into mounds—about 2 tsp/10 mL each. Chill.

4. Melt the remaining chocolate on low heat. Pour into a shallow baking dish. Have another baking dish on hand with the crushed cereal in it. Have another baking sheet lined with waxed paper nearby.

5. Dip the palms of your clean hands lightly into the melted chocolate and roll a cold truffle in the warm chocolate on your hands. Roll the truffle in the crushed cereal and place on the prepared baking sheet. Repeat until all the truffles are rolled.

5. Refrigerate or freeze. I like to serve these at room temperature when the filling is slightly soft inside with a crisp chocolate shell but it's been easy to eat them cold or frozen.

DESSERTS AND PASTRIES

RUSSIAN MOUSSE
WITH STRAWBERRY SAUCE

This creamy concoction has the dairy flavour I adore. If you make it in a heart-shaped mould, it's a perfect dessert for Valentine's Day.

The sauce can also be made with frozen strawberries or raspberries. Use the individually quick-frozen ones for the best results.

SERVES 6 TO 8

RUSSIAN MOUSSE

I	envelope unflavoured gelatine	I
¼ cup	water, cold	50 mL
3	egg yolks	3
⅓ cup	granulated sugar	75 mL
I cup	milk, hot	250 mL
I tsp	pure vanilla extract	5 mL
I cup	sour cream	250 mL
¾ cup	whipping cream	175 mL

STRAWBERRY SAUCE

4 cups	strawberries	I L
¼ cup	granulated sugar	50 mL
¼ cup	Cointreau	50 mL

1. To make the mousse, sprinkle the gelatine over the water in a small saucepan. Allow it to soften for 5 minutes.

2. Beat the egg yolks with the sugar in a saucepan. Beat in the hot milk.

3. Heat the gelatine mixture gently and stir until dissolved. Stir it into the yolk mixture and cook over low heat until slightly thickened, about 5 minutes.

4. Stir in the vanilla and sour cream. Cool until the mixture reaches room temperature.

5. Beat the whipping cream until soft peaks form.

6. Fold the cream quickly into the sour cream base. Pour into a 3-cup/750 mL mould. Cover with plastic wrap and refrigerate for a few hours or overnight.

7. Save a few nice berries for the garnish. Puree the remaining berries with the sugar and Cointreau.

8. Before serving, run a knife around the inside of the mould and invert onto a serving plate. Slice into wedges. Serve with the sauce under or poured over the mousse. Garnish with the reserved berries.

LOWER-FAT VERSION: *Increase sugar to ½ cup/125 mL. Use low-fat sour cream instead of sour cream. Use 1 cup/250 mL yogurt cheese (see page 28) instead of whipping cream.*

AMARETTO TRIFLE

This is a pretty dessert that can easily be made a day ahead. Rum, Grand Marnier or other liqueurs can be used instead of Amaretto.

SERVES 6

CAKE

8 oz	sponge cake (see page 140)	250 g
¼ cup	Amaretto	50 mL
2 cups	strawberries, sliced	500 mL
½ cup	sliced toasted almonds	125 mL

CUSTARD

¼ cup	cornstarch	50 mL
⅓ cup	granulated sugar	75 mL
pinch	salt	pinch
3 cups	milk, cold	750 mL
4	egg yolks	4
½ cup	cream	125 mL
¼ cup	Amaretto	50 mL
1 tsp	pure vanilla extract	5 mL
¼ tsp	almond extract	1 mL

GARNISH

1 cup	whipping cream (optional)	250 mL
2 tbsp	Amaretto (optional)	25 mL

1. Cut the cake into small cubes and spread out in one layer on a cookie sheet or waxed paper. Sprinkle with ¼ cup/50 mL Amaretto.

2. To prepare the custard, combine the cornstarch, sugar and salt in a heavy saucepan. Whisk in ½ cup/125 mL cold milk and blend well. Then add the remaining milk. Cook the custard over gentle heat, stirring constantly, until thickened and mixture just comes to the boil, about 5 minutes.

3. Combine the egg yolks with the cream. Add a little of the hot custard to the yolks to raise the temperature gradually, and then add the yolks to the custard. Cook for a few minutes longer.

4. Stir in ¼ cup/50 mL Amaretto, the vanilla and almond extract. Remove from the heat. Cover with buttered waxed paper to prevent a skin from forming and cool slightly.

5. Divide the cake, sliced strawberries and almonds among large wine glasses or dessert bowls. Pour an equal amount of custard over each serving.

6. To prepare the garnish, beat the whipping cream until stiff. Beat in 2 tbsp/25 mL Amaretto. Pipe or spoon the cream on top of each serving.

LOWER-FAT VERSION: *Omit almonds. Omit cream in custard. Omit the whipped cream garnish. Top each serving with a whole strawberry.*

CHOCOLATE MOUSSE

There are so many chocolate mousse recipes. Try this one and you'll never have to decide again which one to choose!

SERVES 4

4 oz	bittersweet or semisweet chocolate	125 g
¼ cup	unsalted butter	50 mL
2 tbsp	orange liqueur (Cointreau, Grand Marnier or Triple Sec)	25 mL
3	egg yolks	3
½ tsp	pure vanilla extract	2 mL
¾ cup	whipping cream	175 mL

GARNISH

¾ cup	whipping cream, whipped	175 mL
¼ cup	chopped chocolate-coated candied orange peel (optional)	50 mL

1. Melt the chocolate in the top of a double boiler over hot but not boiling water.

2. Beat in the butter until it melts. Add the liqueur and egg yolks and beat thoroughly. Cook gently for a few minutes.

3. Stir in the vanilla. Cool until the chocolate comes to room temperature.

4. Beat ¾ cup/175 mL whipping cream until it is light and soft peaks form. Fold it into the cooled chocolate mixture. Pour the mousse into individual serving dishes and refrigerate for at least 3 hours.

5. Garnish the mousse with whipped cream and the chocolate-coated candied orange peel.

LOWER-FAT VERSION: *Omit the garnish but it will still be very rich.*

COFFEE CRÈME CARAMEL

Some recipes for caramel suggest melting the sugar alone, but I have found that using a little water with the sugar helps to control the crystallization and burning.

SERVES 6 TO 8

CARAMEL

1 cup	granulated sugar	250 mL
¼ cup	water	50 mL

CUSTARD

1 cup	milk	250 mL
2 cups	cream	500 mL
2 tbsp	coffee, coarsely ground	25 mL
2	whole eggs	2
6	egg yolks	6
⅓ cup	granulated sugar	75 mL
2 tsp	pure vanilla extract	10 mL

1. Preheat the oven to 350°F/180°C.

2. To prepare the caramel, place 1 cup/250 mL sugar and the water in a heavy saucepan and stir together well. Heat gently to dissolve the sugar, stirring, then turn up the heat and stop stirring.

3. Cook over high heat for 5 to 10 minutes, or until the caramel turns a golden colour. (Have a small bowl of water and a pastry brush on hand to brush sugar crystals down the sides of the pot.) Slowly pour into a 6-cup/1.5 L soufflé dish. (Make sure the dish you are pouring the hot caramel into is at room temperature. The caramel is very hot and could break a cold dish.) Swirl the caramel in the dish to coat the sides partway up. Reserve.

4. To make the custard, combine the milk, cream and coffee in a saucepan and heat. Cook gently for about 5 minutes. Strain through a cheesecloth- or paper towel-lined sieve.

5. Beat the eggs and egg yolks with ⅓ cup/75 mL sugar. Beat in the milk mixture. Add the vanilla. Strain the custard through a sieve into the caramel-lined pan.

6. Bake the custard in a water bath (a larger pan partially filled with very hot water coming about halfway up the sides of the custard dish) for 40 to 50 minutes, or until set. Cool, then refrigerate overnight.

7. To unmould, run a knife around the edge of the custard and invert carefully onto a dish that has a small lip, to prevent the caramel from leaking over. Serve in wedges with a spoonful of the runny caramel over the top. (You can serve this with whipped cream, but I like it the way it is.) If there is a lot of caramel left in the pan, warm it and pour it over the dessert.

LOWER-FAT VERSION: *There are lots of recipes for lower-fat crème caramel, but I think it's best just to eat less of the real thing. If you do want to try a lower-fat version, however, use 3 cups/750 mL 2% milk instead of regular milk and cream. Use 7 whole eggs in place of 2 whole eggs and 6 yolks.*

BEST RICE PUDDING

When I first described this recipe on the radio 450 people called in for copies. Mailing out the recipe nearly broke the stamp bank! More people have asked for this recipe than any other, and it has been reported that it even saved a marriage! It may sound like a lot of liquid for a little rice, but when it has cooked enough, it will be thick. Trust me.

Short-grain rice is used when you want the finished result to be creamy, so it is usually preferred in dessert recipes.

SERVES 4 TO 6

I cup	water	250 mL
½ cup	short-grain rice	125 mL
5 cups	milk	1.25 L
½ cup	granulated sugar	125 mL
I tsp	cornstarch	5 mL
½ cup	raisins	125 mL
pinch	nutmeg	pinch
I	egg yolk	I
I tsp	pure vanilla extract	5 mL
I tbsp	cinnamon	15 mL
	Cream (optional)	

1. Bring the water and the rice to a boil in a large saucepan for 15 minutes, or until the water is absorbed.

2. Stir 4½ cups/1.125 L milk into the rice and heat gently.

3. Combine the sugar and cornstarch and stir in the remaining ½ cup/125 mL milk. Stir into the rice mixture. Add the raisins and nutmeg.

4. Stirring constantly, bring this to a gentle boil. Reduce the heat to low and cover. Simmer gently for 1 to 1½ hours, or until the pudding has thickened, stirring occasionally. (The time will vary according to the stove and the pot.)

5. When the pudding is thick, add a little to the egg yolk, then beat the yolk into the pudding. Cook gently for another 2 minutes. Remove from the heat and add the vanilla.

6. Spoon the pudding into serving bowls and sprinkle cinnamon over the top. Serve with cream if you are thin. This is good hot or cold, so try it both ways. (The pudding gets even thicker when it cools.)

LOWER-FAT VERSION: *Use low-fat milk. Omit the egg yolk. Do not serve the pudding with cream!*

Frozen Grand Marnier Soufflé with Hot Chocolate Sauce

Many people think you need an ice-cream machine to make homemade ice cream. But this frozen dessert can be made perfectly without one.

SERVES 12

GRAND MARNIER SOUFFLÉ

1 cup	granulated sugar	250 mL
½ cup	water	125 mL
6	egg yolks	6
¼ cup	icing sugar	50 mL
2 tsp	pure vanilla extract	10 mL
½ cup	Grand Marnier or other orange liqueur	125 mL
3 cups	whipping cream	750 mL

HOT CHOCOLATE SAUCE

8 oz	bittersweet or semisweet chocolate	250 g
1 cup	whipping cream	250 mL
2 tbsp	Grand Marnier	25 mL

1. Combine the granulated sugar and water together in a heavy saucepan. Cook, stirring, until the mixture comes to a boil. Continue to cook, without stirring, until the mixture reaches 240°F/115°C on a candy thermometer (and is at the soft ball stage when a bit of the syrup is dropped into a glass of cold water—about 5 to 7 minutes).

2. Meanwhile, beat the egg yolks with the icing sugar until light and fluffy (use a mixmaster or hand mixer for the best results).

3. Slowly drip the sugar syrup into the egg-yolk mixture, beating constantly. Continue to beat the mixture until it is completely cool and very light.

4. Stir in the vanilla and ½ cup/125 mL Grand Marnier.

5. Whip the cream until it is light and forms soft peaks. Gently fold into the Grand Marnier base. Pour the mixture into a 10-inch/25 cm springform pan and cover with plastic wrap. Freeze immediately. When frozen, wrap well if you are planning to keep it for longer than two days.

6. To make the sauce, melt the chocolate and the cream in the top of a double boiler. Beat well until combined thoroughly.

7. Stir in 2 tbsp/25 mL Grand Marnier and serve hot. (The sauce may be prepared ahead, but it will solidify when refrigerated, so warm it again before serving.)

8. Before serving, place the frozen soufflé (if frozen solid) in the refrigerator for 30 minutes to make slicing easier. Run a knife around the inside edge of the springform pan and then unsnap the pan. Serve in wedges and pass the chocolate sauce separately.

RASPBERRY YOGURT MOUSSE

Raspberries are an all-time favourite because of their distinctive sweet-tart taste. Fresh berries are so expensive that although you can use them in this dessert, it's almost best to reserve them for eating on their own. Individually quick-frozen berries can almost always be used interchangeably with fresh in cooked dishes.

If you puree the berries in a food mill, it will also strain out the seeds. If you puree them in a blender or food processor and you do not want the seeds, simply strain the puree. You should have approximately 1 cup/250 mL puree.

SERVES 4 TO 6

1	envelope unflavoured gelatine	1
3 tbsp	water, cold	45 mL
1½ cups	raspberries, pureed	375 mL
¼ cup	granulated sugar	50 mL
1 tbsp	lemon juice	15 mL
2 tbsp	rum	25 mL
½ cup	unflavoured yogurt cheese (see p. 28)	125 mL
1 cup	whipping cream	250 mL

GARNISH

6	fresh raspberries or strawberries	6

1. Sprinkle the gelatine over the water in a medium-sized heavy saucepan. Allow it to soften for 5 minutes. Then heat gently and stir to dissolve.

2. In another saucepan, stir together the raspberry puree, sugar, lemon juice and rum. Heat just until the sugar has dissolved, about 5 minutes.

3. Whisk the raspberry puree into the dissolved gelatine. Cool for 10 minutes.

4. Combine the puree with the yogurt thoroughly. (If the mixture is not at room temperature, cool for a few minutes longer.)

5. Whip the cream until soft peaks form. Fold into the puree. Turn into a large glass serving bowl or individual dessert bowls. Allow to set for 2 hours for individual servings or 4 hours for a large bowl. Garnish with whole berries.

LOWER-FAT VERSION: *Use 1 cup/250 mL additional yogurt cheese in place of whipping cream. Increase sugar to ½ cup/250 mL.*

COFFEE ICE CREAM
WITH CARAMEL SAUCE

Although this sounds simple, the flavour combination is complex and heavenly. Add sliced bananas to make a sundae, or serve the sauce over plain bananas without the ice cream.

Always prepare caramel cautiously—it should be treated with respect. The best caramel is dark brown, but it burns easily, and if that happens it should be discarded. If you use an enamelled pan it is easier to see the colour of the caramel, but as long as the pan is heavy-bottomed, the recipe should work well.

SERVES 4 TO 6

¼ cup	water	50 mL
I cup	granulated sugar	250 mL
I cup	whipping cream	250 mL
2 tbsp	unsalted butter	25 mL
I pint	best-quality coffee ice cream	500 mL

1. Combine the water and sugar in a 3-qt/3 L heavy saucepan. Cook over medium-high heat, stirring, until the sugar dissolves. Continue to cook, but do not stir. Cook until the sugar turns a golden caramel colour. (During the cooking, brush any sugar crystals down the sides of the pan with a pastry brush dipped in cold water.) Do not burn! (If the sugar crystallizes before browning, either add a little more water and cook until it melts, or start again and be careful not to stir after the sugar dissolves.)

2. Remove the pan from the heat and carefully add the cream. Stand back—the mixture will bubble up quite a bit and then settle down, so do not worry. Stir until smooth. (Return to the heat for a minute if necessary to smooth it if the caramel solidifies.)

3. Add the butter and stir to melt. Allow to cool. Serve the sauce with the coffee ice cream. (The sauce can be served warm, at room temperature or cold. As it cools, the sauce will thicken. Store it in the refrigerator.)

LOWER-FAT VERSION: *Replace the whipping cream with ½ cup/125 mL strong coffee, apple juice or orange juice. Omit the butter. Serve the sauce with angel-food cake or fruit instead of ice cream.*

BREAD PUDDING

There are probably as many bread pudding recipes as there are cooks who make it. With the popularity of regional North American cooking and Cajun cooking, it is enjoying quite a revival. Bread pudding is now served in some of the most prestigious restaurants in North America. Chopped pecans, grated coconut, candied fruit or grated chocolate can also be added to this recipe. You can add some or all of these—use about ½ cup/125 mL of each.

SERVES 8

2 tbsp	unsalted butter, at room temperature	25 mL
12	slices bread (preferably brioche or egg bread, crusts on or off)	12
½ cup	raisins or chopped dried apricots	125 mL
⅓ cup	brown sugar	75 mL
1 tbsp	cinnamon	15 mL
¼ tsp	nutmeg	1 mL
6	eggs	6
2	egg yolks	2
⅓ cup	granulated sugar	75 mL
3 cups	milk	750 mL
1 cup	cream	250 mL
1 tsp	pure vanilla extract	5 mL
½ cup	apricot jam	125 mL

1. Butter the bread on both sides. Line the bottom of a 3-qt/3 L casserole dish or oblong baking pan with some of the bread.

2. Combine the raisins, brown sugar, cinnamon and nutmeg. Sprinkle the bread with some of the mixture. Repeat the layers of bread and raisins until everything is used. Top with a layer of bread to prevent the raisins from burning.

3. Beat the eggs and egg yolks with the granulated sugar. Beat in the milk, cream and vanilla. Pour over the bread and allow to stand for 30 to 60 minutes, until the bread has absorbed the custard.

4. Preheat the oven to 350°F/180°C. Bake the pudding for 30 minutes. Check, and if the pudding is browning too much, cover it loosely. Bake for 20 to 30 minutes longer, or until puffed and browned.

5. Heat the apricot jam. Brush it on top of the pudding. Serve warm or cold.

LOWER-FAT VERSION: *Omit the butter and the extra egg yolks. Use low-fat milk and omit the cream.*

Caramelized Applesauce

I love caramel. My husband, Ray, loves apples. This combination is very delicious and pleases us both. You can serve it over ice cream, as a crêpe filling, or as a condiment with goose, duck, roast pork or sausages.

MAKES APPROX. 3 CUPS/750 ML

10	apples (Golden Delicious, Spy or Ida Reds)	10
¼ cup	unsalted butter	50 mL
⅔ cup	granulated sugar	150 mL

1. Peel the apples. Cut them in half and remove the cores. Slice them into slices about ½ inch/1 cm thick.

2. Melt the butter in a large skillet and add the sugar. Cook for approximately 5 minutes. The sugar should begin to melt and turn golden. (Be careful not to burn it.)

3. Add the apples. At first the juices from the apples will come out but eventually, in about 20 minutes, the juices will evaporate and the mixture will start to thicken. The heat should be medium to medium-high. Cook for another 10 minutes, until the apples start to brown and stick—watch them closely and make sure they do not burn. Puree the apples to make a sauce or serve as is.

LOWER-FAT VERSION: *Omit the butter. Melt the sugar in a heavy skillet and add the apples when the sugar browns slightly.*

PEACH FLAMBÉ

Everyone makes a big deal about flambés, but there's really nothing to it. Flambés are done for three reasons—to burn off the alcohol, to singe the top of food (rather like a very quick broil), and for show. In any recipe, if your flambé does not ignite, don't worry. As soon as the mixture is brought to a boil, the alcohol will evaporate anyway. (You want the alcohol to evaporate because raw alcohol can give a slightly bitter taste.) If your flambé doesn't work the first time, try again, but stop there—you can over-liqueur a dish as easily as you can over-salt it. (If you plan to flambé, be sure to turn off any smoke detectors.)

This is a dessert I learned to make when I studied cooking at George Brown College in Toronto and I still love it. It is also delicious made with fresh peaches, pineapple or pears—just use a bit more orange juice or pineapple juice instead of the juices from the can. Serve it with caramel or vanilla ice cream.

SERVES 6

6	peach halves, poached or canned, with the juices	6
½ cup	granulated sugar	125 mL
¼ cup	unsalted butter	50 mL
¼ cup	reserved peach juices (or apricot nectar)	50 mL
¼ cup	orange juice	50 mL
2 tbsp	lemon juice	25 mL
1	cinnamon stick, broken in two	1
4	whole cloves	4
1 tbsp	grated orange peel	15 mL
1 tbsp	grated lemon peel	15 mL
¼ cup	orange liqueur (such as Cointreau)	50 mL
⅓ cup	whipping cream	75 mL
2 tbsp	Cognac	25 mL

1. Drain the peach halves and reserve ¼ cup/50 mL of the juices.

2. Place the sugar in large heavy skillet. Heat until the sugar begins to melt and turn golden. Be careful not to burn it.

3. Add the butter and stir until it has melted. Do not worry if mixture is a bit lumpy at first.

4. Add all the fruit juices, cinnamon stick, cloves and peels. Cook for a few minutes.

5. Add the liqueur and the cream and cook a few minutes longer. Remove the cinnamon and cloves. Add the peaches but cook only until they are heated through.

6. Add the Cognac. Ignite. The idea is to catch the alcohol just as it is evaporating off the surface of the dish. If you are not sure about that precise moment, simply use a long fireplace match and wait for it to ignite.

LOWER-FAT VERSION: *Omit the butter and cream.*

DEEP-DISH APPLE, PEAR AND APRICOT PIE

Years ago, when Trappers restaurant first opened in Toronto, the former owner, Chris Boland, shared this lovely recipe with me, and I still love it. The restaurant was one of the first to emphasize Canadian ingredients.

SERVES 8

FILLING

6	large Spy apples	6
1	large Bartlett pear	1
½ cup	dried apricots	125 mL
2 tsp	lemon juice	10 mL
⅓ cup	granulated sugar	75 mL
2 tbsp	cornstarch	25 mL
1 tsp	cinnamon	5 mL
pinch	nutmeg	pinch

PASTRY

1½ cups	all-purpose flour	375 mL
pinch	salt	pinch
⅓ cup	lard or unsalted butter, cold, cut into bits	75 mL
¼ cup	unsalted butter, cold, cut into bits	50 mL
1	egg	1
¼ cup	water, cold	50 mL

1. Preheat the oven to 400°F/200°C.

2. To make the filling, peel, core and slice the apples and pear. Chop the apricots coarsely (scissors work well).

3. Mix the fruits together and then toss with the lemon juice, sugar, cornstarch, cinnamon and nutmeg. Arrange in a 13- x 9-inch/3 L casserole or baking dish (approximately 3 inches/7.5 cm deep).

4. To make the pastry, combine the flour with the salt. Cut in the lard and butter until they are in tiny pieces.

5. Beat the egg with the water and sprinkle enough over the pastry so that you can gather the dough into a ball. Reserve the remaining egg mixture.

6. Roll out the dough to fit the top of the baking dish. Fit the pastry over the fruit mixture. Brush the top with remaining egg wash and prick the dough with a fork.

7. Bake for 50 to 60 minutes. If the top browns too much, reduce the heat for the last 20 minutes of the baking time. Serve warm.

BLUEBERRY LEMON MOUSSE PIE

Many people think that there's a big secret to making pastry. My students will tell me about a great-aunt who has been making pastry for fifty years and has a secret trick of only using lard. Or a grandmother who has been making pastry for seventy-five years and always uses lemon juice. But the real secret is that these people have been making pastry for a long time. If you only make pastry once a year, you will never get any better. But if you make pastry once a week for even a few months, you will soon be an expert!

This is a rich pastry that uses all butter. It has a wonderful flavour but is very delicate. If it breaks as you're rolling it, simply lift in sections and pat into the pie dish, pressing the edges together.

MAKES ONE 10-INCH/25 CM PIE

CRUST

1½ cups	all-purpose flour	375 mL
pinch	salt	pinch
¾ cup	unsalted butter	175 mL
2 tbsp	vinegar or lemon juice, cold	25 mL

FILLING

1	envelope unflavoured gelatine	1
¼ cup	water, cold	50 mL
3	egg yolks	3
¾ cup	granulated sugar	175 mL
¾ cup	lemon juice	175 mL
1 tbsp	grated lemon peel	15 mL
1 cup	whipping cream	250 mL
2 cups	blueberries (preferably fresh)	500 mL

1. To prepare the pastry, combine the flour with the salt and cut in the butter until it is in tiny pieces. Add the vinegar and gather the dough together to form a ball. Refrigerate for at least 30 minutes.

2. Preheat the oven to 425°F/220°C. Roll out the dough to fit a 10-inch/25 cm pie dish and fit into the pan. Flute the edges. To bake blind, line the dough with parchment paper and fill with pie weights, raw rice or dried beans. Bake for 15 minutes. Remove the rice and paper, etc., and return to 350°F/180°C oven for 15 to 20 minutes to cook through. Watch carefully. Cool thoroughly.

3. To make the filling, sprinkle the gelatine over the cold water in a saucepan. Allow it to rest for 5 minutes. Heat very gently until the gelatine has dissolved.

4. Beat the egg yolks with the granulated sugar until light and lemon-coloured. Beat in the lemon juice and peel.

5. Transfer the mixture to a saucepan and cook until the mixture thickens slightly, about 5 minutes. Stir in the dissolved gelatine. Remove from the heat, transfer the mixture to a bowl and cool until it is at room temperature but not yet set.

6. Beat 1 cup/250 mL cream until soft peaks form. Fold into the cooled lemon mousse.

7. Line the pastry with 2 cups/500 mL blueberries and spread the lemon mousse over the top. Refrigerate for 2 to 3 hours, or until set.

RHUBARB CRISP

I don't think you can beat a rhubarb crisp for a great spring dessert. Serve it with ice cream or whipping cream if you wish. You can also make this with half apples and half strawberries.

SERVES 8

2 lb	rhubarb, trimmed and sliced	1 kg
2 tbsp	unsalted butter, cut into bits	25 mL
¼ cup	granulated sugar	50 mL

TOPPING

¾ cup	all-purpose flour	175 mL
½ cup	brown sugar	125 mL
½ cup	granulated sugar	125 mL
1 tsp	cinnamon	5 mL
½ cup	rolled oats	125 mL
½ cup	unsalted butter	125 mL

1. Preheat the oven to 375°F/190°C.

2. Combine the rhubarb, 2 tbsp/25 mL butter and ¼ cup/50 mL granulated sugar and place in a buttered 13- x 9-inch/3 L casserole dish.

3. Combine the flour, brown sugar, ½ cup/125 mL granulated sugar and cinnamon. Cut in ½ cup/125 mL butter until it is in tiny bits. Blend in the oats. Spread over the rhubarb.

4. Bake for 40 to 50 minutes, or until the rhubarb is tender and the topping is crisp.

LOWER-FAT VERSION: *Use half the butter.*

FRESH PEACH PIE

I don't usually peel peaches for pies or crisps, but if you do want to peel them,
place them in boiling water for 1 minute. Rinse with cold water and peel.
After peeling, pitting and slicing, drain the peaches well before adding them
to the flour and sugar.

This pie is also wonderful made with plums.

MAKES ONE 10-INCH/25 CM PIE

CRUST

⅔ cup	unsalted butter, cold, cut into bits	150 mL
2 cups	all-purpose flour	500 mL
¼ cup	ice water (or more if necessary)	50 mL

FILLING

5 cups	sliced fresh peaches	1.25 L
½ cup	brown sugar	125 mL
½ cup	all-purpose flour	125 mL
1 tsp	cinnamon	5 mL

TOPPING

1	egg	1
1 tbsp	cream	15 mL
1 tbsp	granulated sugar (preferably coarse)	15 mL

1. Preheat the oven to 425°F/220°C.
2. Cut the butter into the flour until the butter is in tiny pieces. Sprinkle with water and gather the dough together into a ball. Use more water only if necessary. Divide the dough in half, with one piece slightly larger than the other.
3. Roll out the larger piece of dough and fit it into a 10-inch/25 cm pie dish.
4. Combine all the ingredients for the filling and place in the pastry-lined dish.
5. Roll out the smaller piece of dough and cut it into strips. Fit the strips across the filling. (For an easy, attractive lattice design, see below.) Crimp the edges.
6. Combine the beaten egg with the cream. Brush the top strips and border of the pie with the glaze. Sprinkle with granulated sugar. Place the pie on a baking sheet.
7. Bake for 15 minutes. Reduce the heat to 350°F/180°C and bake for another 40 minutes.

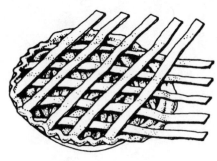

BUTTER TARTS

Although cookbooks often scare pastry makers with their neurotic warnings about over-handling the dough, usually it is okay unless you reroll. If you roll out your pastry and it looks like Norway with the fjords hanging off the sides, don't reroll. It only gets worse, never better.

Making little tarts, however, presents its own problems. You almost have to reroll the scraps to get the right number of tarts. After cutting out the first series of circles, rather than kneading the dough back together into a ball, I gingerly press the scraps together and roll. I rarely reroll the scraps more than once.

MAKES 18 2-INCH/5 CM TARTS

PASTRY

1½ cups	all-purpose flour	375 mL
½ tsp	salt	2 mL
½ cup	unsalted butter, cold	125 mL
¼ cup	water, cold (or more if necessary)	50 mL

FILLING

¼ cup	unsalted butter, at room temperature	50 mL
½ cup	brown sugar	125 mL
1 cup	corn syrup	250 mL
2	eggs	2
1 tsp	pure vanilla extract	5 mL
⅓ cup	raisins	75 mL
⅓ cup	chopped walnuts	75 mL

1. Preheat the oven to 375°F/190°C.

2. To make the pastry, combine the flour and salt. Cut ½ cup/125 mL butter into the flour mixture and sprinkle with the water. Gather the dough together into a ball. Roll out and cut into 2½-inch/6 cm circles. Fit the circles into the tart pans.

3. Blend together the ingredients for the filling, except for the raisins and nuts. Transfer the filling to a measuring cup or container with a spout.

4. Place a few raisins and nuts in each pastry-lined tart. Pour in the filling. Bake on the lowest rack of the oven for 20 to 25 minutes. Cool thoroughly before removing from pans.

CHOCOLATE-COATED STRAWBERRIES

Serve these chocolate-dipped strawberries as a dessert, snack, or as a garnish for chocolate mousse (see page 166). Although they are very easy to prepare, there are a number of tricks that make them even easier.

The berries should be dry when they are dipped into the chocolate. Some berries do not even need washing—wiping with a damp cloth is enough. If they are sandy and need washing, be sure to dry them thoroughly, because a little water could cause the chocolate to seize.

If the strawberry greens are nice, leave the greens on and use them as a handle for dipping. If they are not in good condition, hull the berries and dip the fatter end, grasping the point when dipping.

I like to use European bittersweet chocolate for the berries, but chocolate chips or domestic semisweet will also be fine. Coating chocolate (chocolate that contains more fat and therefore glazes well) can also be used—the finished berries will look shinier, but I prefer the taste of the bittersweet chocolate.

MAKES 15 LARGE STRAWBERRIES

15	large strawberries	15
12 oz	bittersweet chocolate	375 g

1. Clean and dry the strawberries.

2. Melt the chocolate gently over hot water or in the microwave. (When melting chocolate, always remove it from the heat before it is completely melted. Stir to complete the melting. That way there is less chance of burning it.)

3. Dip the strawberries halfway in the chocolate and set them on a waxed paper-lined cookie sheet. Allow them to set in the refrigerator for about 30 minutes.

PEANUT BUTTER MOUSSE PIE

When I was pregnant with Mark, I ate many peanut butter and jam sandwiches every day. People would come into the shop and would always ask what I was eating, expecting it to be something very exotic. I always felt they were terribly disappointed when I told them it was peanut butter and jam. And not even homemade peanut butter or jam.

At first I thought only children would like this pie. And me, of course. But I was wrong. Lots of people love peanut butter.

SERVES 8

CRUST

1 cup	chocolate wafer cookie crumbs (approx. 20 wafers)	250 mL
¼ cup	unsalted butter, melted	50 mL

FILLING

1 cup	peanut butter, smooth or crunchy	250 mL
½ cup	unsalted butter, at room temperature	125 mL
1 cup	granulated sugar	250 mL
1 tsp	pure vanilla extract	5 mL
1½ cups	whipping cream	375 mL
2	Crispy Crunch chocolate bars (45 g each), chopped, or ¾ cup/175 mL chocolate chips	2

1. To make the crust, combine the chocolate wafer crumbs and melted butter. Press into the bottom and sides of a 9-inch/23 cm pie dish.

2. To make the filling, beat the peanut butter with ½ cup/125 mL butter until light and fluffy. Beat in the sugar. Add vanilla and beat well.

3. Beat the cream until soft peaks form. Fold it into the peanut butter mixture with the chopped Crispy Crunch bars or chocolate chips.

4. Mound into the pie shell. Refrigerate for at least 2 hours before serving.

Hot White Chocolate Mocha

This is rich and addictive! When I taught a brunch class at Buffalo Mountain Lodge in Banff last year (the perfect cold place to serve this delicious, warming concoction), we made this for about thirty people in a large saucepan and then frothed it in the espresso machine. There are many commercial hot white chocolate mixes on the market today, but this homemade version to my taste is much better.

SERVES 2

½ cup	chopped white chocolate	125 g
1 tbsp	instant espresso powder	15 mL
1½ cups	hot milk	375 mL
1 tsp	pure vanilla extract	5 mL
	Cinnamon or sifted cocoa	

1. Place the chocolate in a blender. Add the espresso powder, hot milk and vanilla. Blend until frothy.

2. Pour the hot chocolate into mugs and dust with cinnamon or cocoa.

LOWER-FAT VERSION: *Use low-fat milk.*

Index